How to Manage Communication Problems in Young Children

Third Edition

WITHDRAWN

How to Manage Communication Problems in Young Children

Third Edition

Edited by

Myra Kersner and Jannet A. Wright

David Fulton Publishers
London

David Fulton Publishers Ltd
The Chiswick Centre, 414 Chiswick High Road, London W4 5TF
www.fultonpublishers.co.uk

First published in Great Britain in 1993 by Winslow Press
Second Edition 1996, David Fulton Publishers
Third Edition 2002
10 9 8 7 6 5 4 3 2

British Library Cataloguing in Publication Data
A catalogue record for this book is available from the British Library.

ISBN 1 85346 869 X

Typeset by Servis Filmsetting Ltd, Manchester
Printed and bound in Great Britain by The Thanet Press, Margate.

Contents

The third edition of this book is dedicated to Sandy Winyard, friend and colleague, who died in March 2002.

Acknowledgements

We would like to thank Gene Mahon for kindly providing us with the illustrations for Chapter 3.
We would also like to thank Carolyn Bruce for her contribution to Encouraging Language Development, Chapter 9.

Myra Kersner and Jannet A. Wright

Contributors

Monica Bray is a senior lecturer in Speech and Language Pathology and Therapy at Leeds Metropolitan University. Her specialist areas include disfluency and learning disabilities. She is the co-author of *Speech and Language Clinical Process and Practice.*

Renée Byrne is a specialist speech and language therapist working with people who stammer and is the author of *Let's Talk about Stammering.* She is also the adviser to the British Stammering Association.

Myra Kersner is a senior lecturer in the Department of Human Communication Science at University College London. She was responsible for running speech and language courses for nursery nurses, teachers and educational psychologists. She has worked as a speech and language therapist in Yorkshire, London and Toronto, Canada. She is the co-editor with Jannet Wright of *Speech and Language Therapy: The decision-making process when working with children.*

Merle Mahon is a senior lecturer in the Department of Human Communication Science at University College London. She is qualified as a speech pathologist-audiologist and holds an Advanced Clinical Skills Diploma of the College of Speech and Language Therapists in Speech Therapy with Deaf People.

Magdalene Moorey is a senior specialist speech language therapist in south London working in mainstream schools. One of her areas of clinical interest is hearing impairment. She holds the Advanced Clinical Skills Diploma of the Royal College of Speech and Language Therapists.

Rosemarie MorganBarry is a speech and language therapist whose specialist area is children with motor and structural speech disorders. She also works as a freelance lecturer.

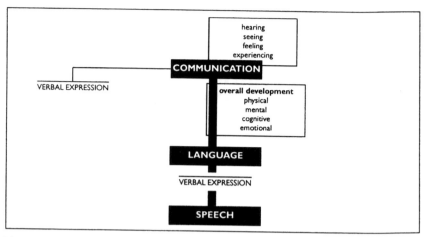

Figure 1.1 The relationship between communication, language and speech

language or speech have developed, and adults in turn communicate with them (see Chapter 2).

From the first day of life, babies receive communication from others, albeit passively, as they begin to see, hear and experience the world around them. When a caring adult holds them close, when they hear words of comfort, or even angry tones, or when they are merely taking part in the feeding process, they are receiving communication from others.

At the same time, babies are able to communicate actively, and express themselves, because, from the day they are born, they are able to tell us when they are wet, hungry or uncomfortable.

There are three basic elements required for expressive communication: **intention, the means,** and **a receiver.**

Intention: this refers to the intention to convey a message. For example babies have the need, almost from the moment of birth, to convey a message expressing their discomfort.

The means: this is the means by which that message may be conveyed. In young babies for example, the means to express their discomfort is by crying.

A receiver: this refers to the person who is required to 'pick up' and respond to the message once it has been sent. With young babies it is usually the parent or carer who hears them crying and is ready to react and respond.

Contributors

Monica Bray is a senior lecturer in Speech and Language Pathology and Therapy at Leeds Metropolitan University. Her specialist areas include disfluency and learning disabilities. She is the co-author of *Speech and Language Clinical Process and Practice.*

Renée Byrne is a specialist speech and language therapist working with people who stammer and is the author of *Let's Talk about Stammering.* She is also the adviser to the British Stammering Association.

Myra Kersner is a senior lecturer in the Department of Human Communication Science at University College London. She was responsible for running speech and language courses for nursery nurses, teachers and educational psychologists. She has worked as a speech and language therapist in Yorkshire, London and Toronto, Canada. She is the co-editor with Jannet Wright of *Speech and Language Therapy: The decision-making process when working with children.*

Merle Mahon is a senior lecturer in the Department of Human Communication Science at University College London. She is qualified as a speech pathologist-audiologist and holds an Advanced Clinical Skills Diploma of the College of Speech and Language Therapists in Speech Therapy with Deaf People.

Magdalene Moorey is a senior specialist speech language therapist in south London working in mainstream schools. One of her areas of clinical interest is hearing impairment. She holds the Advanced Clinical Skills Diploma of the Royal College of Speech and Language Therapists.

Rosemarie MorganBarry is a speech and language therapist whose specialist area is children with motor and structural speech disorders. She also works as a freelance lecturer.

Rachel Rees is a lecturer in the Department of Human Communication Science, University College London. She has worked as a speech and language therapist for many years working closely with nursery nurses, teachers and parents of children with communication difficulties. She has written two chapters in the book *Children's Speech and Literacy Difficulties: Identification and intervention.*

Alison Wintgens is head of speech and language therapy in the Child and Adolescent Mental Health Service, St George's Hospital, London. She specialises in children who have both emotional/behavioural disorders and disorders of communication. She is the co-author of *The Selective Mutism Resource Manual.*

Sandy Winyard lectured extensively on courses for nursery nurses and teachers in the area of speech and language development. She had qualifications in psychology and speech and language therapy.

Jannet A. Wright is a senior lecturer at University College London. As a speech and language therapist she worked with preschool and school-aged children. She is the co-author with Myra Kersner of *Supporting Children with Communication Problems: Sharing the load.*

Introduction

This is the third – and revised – edition of a book which was first published in 1993. The first edition developed from specialist courses that were run in the Department of Human Communication Science, University College London. These courses, which did not assume prior specialist knowledge, aimed to meet the needs of those who wanted to understand the speech and language problems of young children. There were other practitioners however and parents who indicated that they wanted to improve their knowledge and learn more about children's difficulties with communication without attending courses. They wanted a book that was 'jargon-free' and accessible.

Contributors were therefore invited who were specialist speech and language therapists with specific expertise and experience with such children. Some of the chapters have been revised by their original authors, but we are also pleased to introduce Rachel Rees and Monica Bray as new contributors to this third edition.

Learning to talk is something that most children do naturally and without fuss; helping children to communicate and develop speech and language is something that most adults do spontaneously and without thought. There is no need for us to understand this process, the children's role or the adults' role; no reason to know why, or how, speech and language develop – that is, until something goes wrong. It is not until we come across children who are experiencing difficulties, and are not learning to talk, easily and routinely, that we go in search of knowledge. Then we urgently try to find out more about speech and language development, try to discover what has gone wrong, and how we might be able to help put it right.

It is not only parents of young children who might find themselves in this situation. Nursery nurses, assistants, volunteers as well as teachers of young children may find that they are working with children with speech, language and communication difficulties and they too welcome information regarding communication problems.

The aim of the book is to offer some insight and understanding into some of these difficulties: to indicate what signs to look out for; to offer some interpretation of what these signs might mean; to suggest how best to help, and where and how to seek expert advice. In this third edition we have made additions and alterations to reflect new developments and current practice. For example, the material in the book is relevant to practitioners who may be following the Early Learning Goals or working on Sure Start programmes. Similarly, increased access to the Internet has meant that we have been able to include web site addresses for relevant organisations and resources.

We hope that this third edition will continue to be a useful text for fellow professionals. It may also be helpful for those who are contemplating a career working with young children by highlighting some of the problems they will encounter. In addition, we hope that parents will continue to find it a useful resource. We hope that it will help them to understand more fully their children's difficulties, and thus enable us all to work together for the benefit of the children in our care.

Myra Kersner and Jannet A. Wright

Chapter 1

How to Manage Communication Problems in Young Children

Myra Kersner

The children described in this book are, in the main, the kind of children who may be found in any nursery or a mainstream classroom. They may have a variety of different types of communication problems. In order to understand these problems it is helpful to understand about how communication develops.

Speech, **language** and **communication** are words which most of us use, comfortably and often, taking for granted that we understand their meaning. However, as with many words, there can be different aspects to their meaning, according to different contexts, and, when they are used in a professional context by speech and language therapists, they take on a specific meaning. This book has been written by speech and language therapists, and, throughout the text, these three words are referred to in their technical sense, in terms of the developing child. It is important therefore that they should be clearly defined at the outset, and that the relationship between them in this context be explained (see Figure 1.1).

Figure 1.1 illustrates how communication develops as the new-born baby sees, hears and begins to experience the world. Initially the baby communicates using **non-verbal expression** such as crying, laughing or cooing. As the child begins to develop physically, cognitively and emotionally, so the understanding of language develops. This language may then be communicated using **verbal expression** or **speech**. (This is more fully developed in Chapter 2.)

Communication

Communication is about receiving and expressing messages. It is generally defined in terms of social interaction – people talking to each other. However, it is more than that. Communication may occur without people talking; for instance, new-born children communicate long before

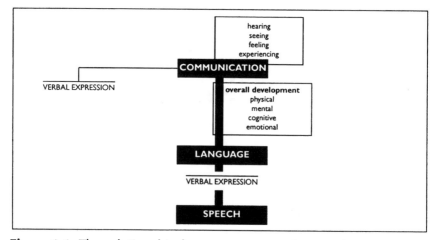

Figure 1.1 The relationship between communication, language and speech

language or speech have developed, and adults in turn communicate with them (see Chapter 2).

From the first day of life, babies receive communication from others, albeit passively, as they begin to see, hear and experience the world around them. When a caring adult holds them close, when they hear words of comfort, or even angry tones, or when they are merely taking part in the feeding process, they are receiving communication from others.

At the same time, babies are able to communicate actively, and express themselves, because, from the day they are born, they are able to tell us when they are wet, hungry or uncomfortable.

There are three basic elements required for expressive communication: **intention, the means**, and **a receiver**.

Intention: this refers to the intention to convey a message. For example babies have the need, almost from the moment of birth, to convey a message expressing their discomfort.

The means: this is the means by which that message may be conveyed. In young babies for example, the means to express their discomfort is by crying.

A receiver: this refers to the person who is required to 'pick up' and respond to the message once it has been sent. With young babies it is usually the parent or carer who hears them crying and is ready to react and respond.

These three elements of communication are usually in place at birth, and it is from this cycle that early **communication patterns** are set (see Figure 1.2).

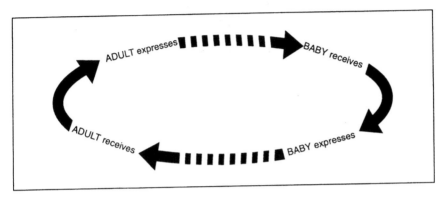

Figure 1.2 Communication patterns

As Figure 1.2 illustrates, the baby expresses discomfort by crying; the adult carer receives that message and responds, perhaps with soothing words or noises; the baby hears these noises and responds, perhaps with a modified type of expression such as a whimper, or a comfort noise. It is also important to notice that when an adult receives the baby's first message she or he will probably respond, in addition, with an action, such as feeding the baby, or changing its nappy. This action will reinforce the baby's intention to communicate, because the baby will realise that its attempts to communicate are rewarded by adults' actions.

At first babies are only able to communicate their feelings of discomfort, but gradually they begin to signal: 'I am happy; I am comfortable' by cooing, gurgling, or smiling, and the cycle once again is reinforced. Normally, this repertoire of pre-language, non-verbal forms of expression increases as children develop more understanding of language, until finally, they are ready to speak (see Chapter 2).

Language

Although communication begins at birth, language does not develop until the child begins to grow and mature, absorbing sensory experiences from the outside world. Language is extremely complex, although, once acquired, we use it extensively and automatically (Syder 1992). The very young baby, however, 'is motivated to be a good communicator, so that by the time language comes "on line" at around the first birthday, most of the basic capacity to use it has already developed' (Law 1992).

Language is a form of shorthand, which is used as a means of classifying and ordering the world. Various symbols are used to represent objects, situations, and the everyday occurrences of life. These symbols are the spoken, written or signed words, which, over generations, have evolved (and continue to evolve) into an agreed and accepted system of symbols – a particular language. For example spoken or written English is a system of symbols governed by over 1,000 grammatical rules (Crystal 1986) that are accepted and recognised both in this country and by many people throughout the world. Adults may be expected to have about 50,000 different words that they are able to use, and they will often understand and recognise up to twice that number (Crystal 1986).

As young children begin to understand the symbols of their own language, gradually, they are able to use that language to express their own messages and to improve their communication. It is surprising to realise how many words may be used even by young children. A study cited in Crystal 1986 shows that at 17 months one child was able to use 1,860 words of different types. These included nouns, naming people and different categories of objects; verbs, describing a variety of actions; descriptive words referring to location, and words such as 'more' and 'again'.

The use of language means that a greater variety of messages may be communicated to larger numbers of people. Language allows messages to be more precisely expressed, so that they will be easily understood. For example, the mother of a 15-month-old boy may understand that when he says: 'er ber ber' and points his finger, he means, 'There's a bus over there', but she may be the only person who understands this. However, anyone who understands English will know what he means once he is able to say the words: 'Look, there's a bus.' By the time the child is five, he may be expected to use over 2,400 different words (Crystal 1986).

Language may be expressed in a variety of ways (see below). Most commonly however, it is expressed through words that are spoken out loud.

Speech

Speech may be thought of as verbal expression, and it is the mechanism by which most people communicate. Speech requires the use of the voice to make sounds. In English these sounds are then formed and shaped by the tongue, lips, teeth and palate to make the 20 vowel sounds and 24 consonant sounds which are then combined in over 300 different ways to form English words (Crystal 1986). When these words are heard and recognised by others, they respond with other words; thus the links between speech, language and communication are formed and the relationship is completed. How this relationship develops is explained in detail in the next chapter.

Other ways of expressing language

There are other ways in which language may be expressed non-verbally. As Figure 1.3 shows, as well as using speech, language may be expressed using two other forms of non-verbal expression: **non-vocal expression** and **body language**.

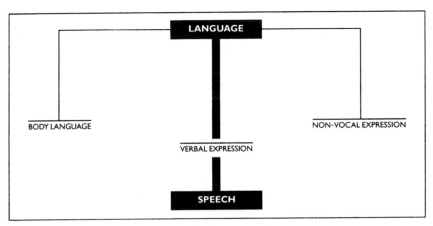

Figure 1.3 Verbal and non-verbal expression

Non-vocal expression

There are several forms of non-vocal expression. One way is to use written symbols (letters), which can be written down and read. Reading and writing as a form of expression is usually learned after speech has developed, when children go to school.

There are some children however, who may understand language, but whose speech does not develop properly; they have to learn to express their language in other ways. This may occur with children who have hearing problems, or with some of those who have learning disabilities; it may be that they have a physical disability, such as cerebral palsy, or they may have a specific problem affecting the speech organs such as paralysis or a degenerative disease.

In such cases these children may be taught an alternative system of communication such as a sign language (British Sign Language), a symbol system where they point to pictures, words or specific symbols (Makaton Symbols or Blissymbols – see Glossary), or they may use written words if they are able to read and write.

In some cases, a technical aid such as an electronic communication device, or a speech synthesiser, may provide an alternative to speech (Clarke *et al.* 2001).

Body language

Body language is yet another example of non-verbal expression. These messages, however, which may be sent either consciously or unconsciously, are usually used in addition to the spoken word. This form of non-verbal expression amplifies speech, giving it another dimension, sometimes even another meaning.

An example of body language is making eye contact, or alternatively avoiding someone's gaze. This gives unspoken messages about the level of confidence, shyness, awkwardness or embarrassment which one may be feeling during a particular interaction.

Stance gives another message. The arms akimbo position of fists on the waist with the elbows pointing outwards is often considered to look aggressive, whereas the arms folded across the chest may be interpreted as defensive.

Gestures may help to emphasise a spoken message, such as wagging a finger while telling someone off. Gestures may even replace the spoken word, such as when pointing, or shrugging the shoulders.

Different facial expressions also give additional messages. Smiling or frowning may quickly convey an accurate message regarding feelings, which may help to underline the words of the message.

However, facial expressions may also be used to convey 'a mixed message'. This may occur for example when the speaker uses an angry voice, which is belied by a twinkle of the eye, or when seemingly harmless words are combined with a sarcastic lifting of the eyebrows. Such non-verbal messages play an important role in communication.

Difficulties with communication

Sometimes, however, the ideal relationship between communication, speech and language is not achieved. The links are not made and communication, at some level, breaks down. In such instances, children may be said to have a 'communication disorder' which is an 'umbrella term' covering a wide range of difficulties concerning speech, language and communication (Syder 1992). It is recognised that as many as 5 per cent of children enter school with some of these difficulties. It would therefore seem to be important for nursery nurses, teachers and care workers to ensure that they have an understanding of children's speech and language problems. Indeed, because more children with special educational needs now enter mainstream schools, more education staff require knowledge and skills in the management of children with speech and language difficulties. The relationship between communication, language and speech is a complex one and the ability to communicate is dependent on the social and emotional as well as the physical environment (Syder 1992). It is therefore possible that it could break down at any stage during a child's development. The effect this would have on the young child would depend at which level of this relationship the breakdown occurred.

For example, if something went wrong during the early stages of development, before the patterns of communication were fully established, this could result in the child having difficulties in the subsequent development of language, and later, speech. If, conversely, there was for example a physical problem affecting the organs of speech, this would not necessarily affect language development or the establishment of communication patterns.

Describing children's speech and language

Which terms to use to describe children's abnormal speech and language development is often a point for discussion among speech and language therapists. For example, there is debate, but not always agreement, regarding the use of terms such as 'disordered' and 'delayed': when should one be used, when the other? This text does not attempt to make such distinctions. In the following chapters, such words as 'delayed'; 'disordered'; 'difficulties'; 'problems' and 'impairment' are used interchangeably.

However, it is always advisable to discuss such terms with your speech and language therapy colleagues, to ensure that they are being used in the same way by all those working together with any particular child.

While it may not be important to differentiate the terminology, it is important to be able to recognise children who have problems; to be able to classify broadly the area in which they (the children) are having the most difficulty – is it with language? with speech? or with basic patterns of communication? – and to know how to begin to help. If children are not given such help at the appropriate time the overall effect may be that their communicative skills may not be learned at the appropriate time, or may not be learned at all.

The population of children

Children with communication problems may be found in any nursery or a mainstream classroom. They may not appear different from other children and yet they may be experiencing some difficulties with speech/language/communication. These are the children who are often in danger of being overlooked, if their particular difficulty is not understood. There are several reasons that might account for their speech and language difficulties, some of which will be dealt with in the following chapters. These include: hearing difficulties; speech and language problems; emotional and behavioural problems; and stammering.

Hearing difficulties

Babies are normally able to hear at least from the moment of birth. If there are difficulties with this fundamental sensory system, it can be seen from Figure 1.1 how the entire communication system and the development of language and speech may be affected to some degree. Some children may enter school with a hearing problem, because carers have not been able to recognise the problem, or have not known what to do about it if a loss was suspected. Details of how hearing difficulties may affect the young child are described in Chapter 3.

Speech and language problems

Although diagnosis of specific speech and language disorders requires the specialist knowledge of a speech and language therapist, nursery nurses, teachers and care workers are often able to recognise and describe children's communication problems. There is a description and discussion in Chapter 4 of how to recognise and distinguish some of these difficulties. For example, how to recognise problems in the communication patterns described in Figure 1.2; how to recognise difficulties with understanding language; and how to recognise some expressive language and articulation difficulties, such as the development of certain sounds.

Stammering

Stammering is a specific problem affecting the speech and language of people of all ages. As many as 5 per cent of the population have stammered at some time in their lives (Bloodstein 1995). Although fewer children are affected by stammering than by other disorders, stammering may sometimes prove more difficult to manage than some articulation problems. Stammering affects verbal expression, the speech and language output, which may sound as if it were 'broken up' and not fluent. The problems that arise with children who stammer, and how they may be helped, are dealt with in Chapter 5.

Emotional and behavioural difficulties

Although emotional difficulties may arise as a result of speech and language problems, and the resultant frustration of having an impaired communication system, it can be seen from Figure 1.1 that emotional development plays an important role in the development of the child as a whole, and particularly in the development of language and speech. Some emotional and behavioural difficulties may also contribute to communication and/or language difficulties. This is discussed more fully in Chapter 6.

The involvement of the speech and language therapist

Wherever possible it is best to seek the advice of a speech and language therapist, to discuss the ways in which to help any child with a communication difficulty, even if the therapist is not able to see the child regularly. The role of the speech and language therapist is not always understood and Chapter 7 has been included in order to explain this role and how children may be referred.

How can you help?

The development of language and speech is an intrinsic and integral part of the development of the child as a whole, and there are many ways in which children can be helped if they are experiencing difficulties with this aspect of their development. Chapter 8 contains suggestions for enhancing language development by discussing formal language 'programmes'. There are also many games and activities which are useful for such children which teachers could incorporate into their curriculum planning or which could become part of the routine in a nursery or at home. Ideas and suggestions for the inclusion of these informal activities are given in Chapter 9.

Working with parents

It is acknowledged that parents are often among the first to recognise that something is wrong with their child; it is therefore important for them to be included in the helping process, whenever possible. How professionals may approach and facilitate this aspect of their work is discussed in the final chapter.

There are, of course, many other groups of children who have speech and language difficulties who are beyond the scope of this book. Mostly these are children who have communication disorders as a result of other disabilities such as cerebral palsy, or other physical disabilities; severe or mild learning disabilities or have been diagnosed as autistic. Many of these children may need specific specialist help.

Further reading

Cumine, V., Leach, J. and Stevenson, G. (2000) *Autism in the Early Years.* London: David Fulton Publishers.

Fawcus, M. (1997) *Children with Learning Difficulties.* London: Whurr Publishers.

Finnie, N. (1997) *Handling the Young Cerebral Palsied Child at Home,* 3rd edn. London: William Heinemann.

Chapter 2

The Development of Communication – Speech and Language Acquisition

Sandy Winyard

As has been shown in Chapter 1, the process of communicating starts from birth, and the development of communication into language and speech begins as the new-born baby draws its first breath.

Communication is an **interactive process**; that means more than one person is involved. Even from birth it is something that does not occur alone, it is dependent on other factors, such as people and events. This can be illustrated by thinking about any conversation. What one person says is dependent on what the other person says; on their reactions to the first person's communication.

Communication is both verbal and non-verbal. The verbal part of the communication is the words that are spoken. The non-verbal part consists of facial expression, such as smiling and frowning; eye contact; and gestures, such as beckoning, pointing, or waving. Body language also provides non-verbal information for the listener. For example, slouching and turning away from someone indicates disinterest and boredom, while sitting up straight and turning towards someone indicates interest and attention. Normally, communication requires both verbal and non-verbal skills and it is important to remember that much information is conveyed by both methods.

Language development

Language can be divided into **expression** and **comprehension**. Expression is what children say or do that conveys what they want to communicate. Comprehension is what children understand from verbal messages, when they are spoken to, and what they understand from what is conveyed in a non-verbal way by gestures and/or body language.

Language can be described by breaking it down into several parts.

Sounds

The sounds in spoken English do not match the letters of the alphabet. For example:

- the letter 'a' is pronounced differently in the words: 'pan'; 'pane'; 'park';
- the 'sh' sound in words like 'shop' and 'shape', although it is said as one sound it is written with two letters from the alphabet;
- 'cat' is written with three letters and has three sounds c–a–t, but 'sharp' has five letters and three sounds sh–ar–p.

When children are learning to talk, it is the sounds that are learnt, not the letters. It is these sounds with which they sometimes have problems (see Chapter 4).

Content

This is the words or **vocabulary** which make up the meaning of a message; that is, what children want to convey. Children may sometimes try to convey the same message as an adult, but the way that they say it may sound different. Child language is different from adult language. It is not incorrect or wrong, rather it is developing.

Some children may pronounce the words incorrectly. For example, they may confuse some sounds in words so that they say 'tat' instead of 'cat', or 'gog' instead of 'dog'.

Their sentences may be incomplete. For example: 'Daddy sock,' may mean 'Daddy I want my sock,' or 'This is Daddy's sock.'

The order of the words may be incorrect. For example, a child may say 'Go car me' instead of 'Me go car' meaning 'I want to go in the car.'

However, despite sounding different, the message may still be clear to the listener because **contextual clues** may be given; that is information that will help the understanding of the message. This may come from the general situation, or from previous knowledge and information known to the two people who are communicating.

For example, Tom asks his mother: 'Where loon?' What he means is, 'Where is the balloon?'

His mother's interpretation of this is dependent on her knowledge of his language and her knowledge of her child and his environment. His mother may know that he has been playing with a balloon, or that he has called it a 'loon' previously; or she may have been told about it by someone who has seen the balloon game. Because she has this information, the mother can understand what Tom is talking about.

Grammar

This refers to the rules of language. The words that express ideas, give information and convey feelings are not put together in a haphazard way. They are organised into structured sentences according to grammatical rules. These rules of language are sometimes referred to as **syntax**.

For example, when describing the size and colour of an object in English, size always comes before the colour. Thus we say a 'big, blue ball', not a 'blue, big ball'.

In summary: language comprises sounds, which combine to make words, which combine to make sentences.

Use

Language fulfils a variety of communication functions such as greeting people, asking questions, explaining a problem, or telling a story. The **use** of language or **pragmatics** refers to the way language, both verbal and non-verbal, is used appropriately in different social situations. For example, children use language in a more informal way when talking to their friends than when talking to their teachers. The majority of children learn spontaneously how to use language appropriately. For example they learn how to take turns in conversations; they learn how to start a conversation, how to end it, how to keep it going and how to change the topic in an appropriate way.

Intonation

This means the rising or falling sound patterns of speech, or the melody. Intonation has an important role in communication because it is this melody that is one of the first features of speech and language that children both understand and produce. The intonation carries much of the information about the content or meaning of a message.

For example, if the sentence 'We're going out' is said as a statement, announcing the intention to go out, the intonation usually goes down so that the voice will drop at the end. Try saying it.

The same sentence can be turned into a question by changing the intonation pattern. For a question, the intonation rises at the end. Now try saying 'We're going out?' as a question. Can you hear the difference?

Young children rely on the information provided by intonation patterns to help them understand what is said, long before they understand the individual words in a sentence they hear.

Voice

Voice is produced when yelling, shouting, or speaking. The air that is breathed in is forced out of the lungs through the mouth and/or nose. This stream of air passes through the vocal cords or vocal folds situated in the neck. Try putting a finger on your Adam's apple, the lump of cartilage on the front of your neck; the vocal cords or **larynx** are within this protuberance. Say 'bbb'. You will feel vibrations. This is because the vocal cords are vibrating as the air passes through them.

Children frequently use a loud voice, and at school they often shout in the playground. It is possible for their voices to become hoarse because of excessive shouting. If hoarseness persists, then they may need to be seen by a speech and language therapist to help them use their voices less stridently.

The same can happen to adults, especially teachers who have to project their voices over a noisy classroom. They may strain their voices and become hoarse. They may even 'lose' their voice. If this happens, they too may need help from a speech and language therapist, or from a doctor, or an ear, nose and throat (ENT) specialist.

How do children learn language?

Imitation

If asked how children learn language, some people would say, by imitation – they hear words and copy them. There is no doubt that some of the words children produce are imitated. For example, three-year-old Sam was overheard saying to his best friend, 'You can't have ice cream until you've eaten your dinner.' He used exactly the same words, as well as the voice and intonation pattern that his mother used to him a few days earlier. This is a clear example of imitation.

However, imitation cannot tell the whole story about how children learn to speak. Even allowing for the fact that children hear many different examples of language, from many different sources, such as at home, with friends or at school, imitation cannot account for the new and original ways in which children then produce and use language themselves.

If children learned to speak only by imitation we would expect children's speech to be the same as adults' speech. However, as we saw before, the language of the child is not a replica of the language of an adult – it is different. It seems to have its own patterns and to follow its own rules.

No matter how often you say, 'Daddy has just gone to work in the car,' children can only attempt to repeat such a sentence using the language that corresponds to the level or stage of their development. For example, in the case of two and a half-year-old Tom, his attempted repetition of this sentence was, 'Daddy go work car.'

Another way children's speech differs from adults' speech is that children do not indulge in 'babytalk' in the way many adults do. For example, how many children refer to their toes as 'piggy wiggys'?

Another argument against imitation is that, by adult standards, children's language is full of errors. For example, children talk about 'mouses' – they do not immediately imitate the word 'mice'. Similarly they use 'goed' instead of 'went' and 'badder' instead of 'worse'. This is quite normal – all children go through these stages while they are developing language. The rate at which they develop may vary, some take longer than others to progress through the stages of 'child language' to mature language structures.

Innate ability

If imitation does not explain how language develops, then how do children develop language? There are some researchers such as Chomsky (1959) who feel that children are born with an innate ability to produce language. The language they are exposed to in their environment, which they hear all around them, then triggers this inbuilt ability.

This theory certainly offers an explanation as to how children are able to learn a limited number of words and use them in combinations they have obviously never heard before.

These two approaches focus on the child rather than the people who communicate, or interact with the child, whereas the interaction approach outlined below focuses on the way that adults and children communicate together.

Adult–child interaction and the development of language

This approach focuses on the person in conversation with the child, for example the mother, and is thought to be important in the development of language. Work on this approach was based on original research by

Bruner (1975). Here, the mother's contribution or **input** is thought to be fundamental to the child's normal development of speech and language.

Viewed from the perspective of the child, language development in terms of adult–child interaction may be considered in two stages – pre-verbal and verbal.

Pre-verbal stage

The pre-verbal stage covers the period from babies' first cries to the emergence of their first words. The adults' input during this stage is important because, initially, it is the way adults respond to the cries and physical actions of babies that give those cries and actions meaning. A baby who wriggles, kicks and cries could be trying to communicate:

'I'm hungry';
'I'm uncomfortable and wet and want to be changed';
'I want to be picked up and made a fuss of.'

The adult interprets the meaning by responding to the baby's behaviour, for example by offering food, changing a dirty nappy, or picking up and cuddling the infant. The way the adult responds will influence the child's behaviour.

In this way children learn that some of their messages mean something to the adults around them, and that some of their messages are ignored and need to be altered before the adults will respond in the required way.

Of course, this can be a two-way process and sensitive adults learn from the babies' responses whether they have responded appropriately to the messages.

During this pre-verbal stage babies spend a great deal of time practising the sounds and melodies of speech. They will make noises, their mothers will often make the same noises back. This is one of the ways in which babies learn the **turn-taking skills** required for later stages in their language development, when they need to learn how to use language in social contexts and to take turns in verbal conversations.

Listening and attention

In order to interact in this way young children have to be able to listen and pay attention, and, long before they can talk, they will listen and attend when an adult is talking. Listening and attending is more than just hearing, it is more than just being aware of noises and happenings all around; it involves actively concentrating on the noises in the environment. Babies demonstrate that they are really listening by focusing on the adult's face and stopping all activity while the adult is talking. When the adult stops talking they start to make noises and thrash around with their limbs as they 'take their turn' in the conversation.

By about nine months children realise that they can influence adult behaviour by using various communication strategies like gestures, vocalisations, or even by making eye contact. This may be considered to be intentional behaviour because children really want the particular message they are sending to be understood. They know what they are trying to communicate and are sending signals using the same combination of sounds, gestures or looks that in the past have achieved the responses they want from the adult.

For example, baby Ben, at 11 months, knows that the sounds 'erer' said with a certain intonation, together with a pointing gesture, will always result in him getting a drink. Therefore he will reproduce it next time he wants a drink.

Child-directed speech

When interacting with young babies, adults employ a different sort of communication style. This child-directed speech tends to be simpler than the speech used when talking to an adult; and, while the sentences are correct in grammar and sounds, they tend to be short and simple in their construction. Speech is often slower, louder, and on a higher note; and words that the adult really wants the child to understand are emphasised by putting more stress on them, for example: 'Tom, go and get the ball, get the *ball.*'

Vocal play

While building turn-taking skills with their mother or father, babies still have time for practising their speech, by playing with sounds. They progress from crying and making basic sounds through happy, cooing noises to vocal play. Vocal play is quite melodic and babies often bang toys in time with their vocalisations. This stage is reached at about four months.

For example, Sophie was four months old when she began to produce a greater variety of sounds – vowel sounds like 'ah' and 'oo' and 'oh' and consonant sounds like 'g', 'k', 'm' became common. She produced one sound and then repeated it over and over again. She also produced trills and blew 'raspberries'. All of these are common features at this age, and are typical of vocal play.

Babbling

At about six months the babbling stage begins. Most people are familiar with this and remember the long strings of 'babababab' or 'dadadadada' which infants produce. As the baby continues to babble, the sounds become more varied and change within the string, so that strings like 'madumadu' may be produced.

Jargon

At about nine months the intonation patterns of speech are picked up more intensely and practised. Gradually the length of sounds produced by children increases and they sound as if they are producing adult speech. In fact, they are not using real words, they are producing strings of sounds with intonation patterns they have learnt from adults. This is called jargon.

By the end of this phase, children are ready to enter the verbal stage. They have acquired many **functional communication skills**: they have learnt the conversational skills of turn-taking, listening and attending; they have practised using their voice, different intonation patterns and sounds; they have practised using some content, and getting their message across to their listener. They continue to practise these functional communication skills, by making their needs known, and manipulating their world by intentionally communicating. They have begun to realise the power of language and they have not yet said a word!

Verbal stage

Into this non-verbal framework of sounds and intonation, the child, at about 12 to 15 months, begins to insert words. The first words children say are usually the names of things that are in their personal world which are important to them. The first words might be, 'cup', 'bear', 'car', 'drink', names of the family, or pets. These words may not be pronounced perfectly; for example, cup might be 'cu' or drink might be 'dint' or 'dink'. However, by this stage, the word is always used to mean the same thing, showing that the child has attached meaning to it and is using it consistently to convey the same message.

Generalisation

Sometimes children use the same word to mean a number of things that seem similar to them. So, the word 'dog', for a period in the child's language development, might be used for all the four-legged animals the child comes across, such as dogs, cats and horses. A common example of this **generalisation** is the use of the word 'Daddy' or 'Mummy'. Once learnt, 'Daddy' may then be used for all men, and 'Mummy' for all women. A similar process may also happen with the name of the family pet. It is very common to hear a child calling everybody's cat 'Smokey' because that is the name of their own cat. Gradually children learn to refine these 'umbrella' terms or generalisations and learn, for example, that a cat is different from a dog. They also learn that not all men are Daddy.

The 'two-word' stage

A little later in their development – from approximately two years upwards – children begin to put two words together. These two-word phrases or sentences are the beginnings of real grammar and may represent a number of different functions like statements, requests and questions.

For example:

'Car gone,' is a statement meaning, 'The car has gone.'

'Mummy biscuit?' is a request meaning, 'Mummy, please may I have a biscuit?'

'Where train?' – spoken with a rising inflection – is a question meaning, 'Where is the train?' or, 'Where has the train gone?'

These are examples of how children are able to get their message across, successfully, to their listeners using a restricted and immature grammar or rule system, and knowing only a small number of words.

How the listener interprets the meaning of the child's language is important. For example, when two-year-old Samantha says a phrase like, 'Mummy shoe' she might mean:

'Mummy, where's my shoe?' (a question);

or, 'Mummy, where's your shoe?' (a question);

or, 'Mummy, here's your shoe' (a statement);

or, 'Mummy, here's my shoe' (a statement).

The intonation pattern will reveal whether she meant the words to be a question or a statement. But, whether she meant it to refer to her mother's shoe or to her own shoe will be revealed by contextual clues, such as the general situation, or by other language that has been used before or after the phrase in question.

A child may want to convey a number of different messages by using the same two words, and it is only by understanding the situation and listening to the intonation pattern that the listener can make the correct interpretation. This illustrates how the listener helps the child to expand his/her language skills. The listener does this by understanding the message the child is trying to communicate as well as by using other clues such as the intonation pattern, the environment and any gestures the child may use to help communication. The listener shows that they have understood by responding appropriately.

Acknowledging, reinforcing, modelling and expanding

Adults help children to develop their language skills by acknowledging that they have said something, reinforcing what they have said and modelling a correct or mature response. They may also expand what children have said, providing more information about the subject, so that children's vocabulary and knowledge of the language grows.

For example, Katherine, aged two and a half, and her mother are out shopping in the high street one day. Katherine suddenly says: 'Mummy, bu', pointing at the bus. Her mother replies appropriately: 'Yes, it's a bus' (reinforcing and modelling). She then expands: 'A big, red bus with people on. We could go on a bus to see Granny tomorrow. Would you like that?'

Katherine's mother has provided acknowledgement, by saying, 'Yes'. She has reinforced and provided the correct model, by repeating what Katherine has said, but using the adult form, 'bus' instead of 'bu'; and she has expanded what Katherine said by telling her more about it. This will encourage Katherine to keep the conversation going, because her mother showed interest in what she was talking about. Her mother did not introduce a new subject; she followed Katherine's lead by talking about her choice of subject. If she is responded to in this way, Katherine should feel good about communicating and hopefully will continue to do so.

These strategies can be particularly useful if children are having difficulty learning to talk. Then the adults around them have to become aware of strategies which they may have used previously, unconsciously, and try to use them intentionally in order to encourage language development.

If you think about how you communicate with children, you probably do this quite naturally most of the time. Try and be aware of the messages you are giving to the children you talk to. Are you encouraging, like Katherine's mother in the example above? Or could your messages sound discouraging? This could be conveyed, for example, by not acknowledging what the child has said, or by changing the subject to one of your own choice.

Gordon Wells (1985) suggested that children practise language skills with children of their own age, but learn language from people who are older and who are skilled language users themselves.

Concept development

At the same time as language is developing, young children are developing concepts. These help children to put some order into their world and to understand the world around them. Concept development may be reflected in their use of language, although the stages of development of concepts and language do not always coincide.

Possession

Once the child understands the concept of possession the word 'mine' may be used a great deal, although not always appropriately, such as in 'Mine teddy', 'Mine cup'. The word 'yours' may be used, but again, probably inappropriately at first, because the concept of sharing one's possessions with someone else is not yet understood.

Position

Similarly, when children begin to use words which indicate position, for example: 'in'; 'on'; 'under', the ability to use such words correctly is linked to their intellectual development. Children will begin to use the words in phrases such as 'doll in chair', 'cup on table' long before they have understood that 'in'; 'on'; 'under' refer to a specific position.

Size, shape, colour

The words indicating the size, shape or colour of an object may be used at first in imitation, without any real understanding of what they mean. As children begin to understand the concept of size and shape, they may begin to use the words appropriately, for example: 'Dat big cup', 'My big bed'. Between their third and fourth birthday they will begin to recognise and name colours as in: 'Where yellow ball?'

The understanding and use of position words and vocabulary to describe size and colour gives children a more precise grasp of language. When asking for a special cup from the top shelf in the kitchen, they can now say, 'Red one,' which is much quicker and more efficient than saying, 'Dat one,' and pointing. Although previously the message would have been understood, it might have taken longer to convey the same information, depending on the number of choices available. Children quickly learn how useful it is to be more precise with language, and may well practise their new skills by demanding all sorts of things.

Adults also enjoy children's growing language skills as it means they no longer have to spend as much time working out the meaning of what children are saying. Communication is quicker and more fun, with new vocabulary being used all the time. As children are more involved in tasks in the home and actually experience activities such as washing up, hoovering, making the beds and fixing broken objects they will talk about them at the same time. This gives them the best possible experience of language at its most meaningful.

The development of grammatical structure

By the third year, children are quite sophisticated language users, able to make statements and describe things, ask questions and claim possession appropriately. The third year is often thought of as the one when most linguistic progress occurs, although to the adult listener the child's speech is full of grammatical errors. For example, word endings are often incorrect.

Tenses

When trying to form the past tense of a regular verb, such as walk, jump, want, children work out that there is a rule about adding '-ed', when talking about what they did yesterday. They will then over-generalise this new rule, adding '-ed' to all verbs, even irregular ones where this rule does not apply, producing words like:

'I goed' or 'wented' instead of 'I went';
'I runned' instead of 'I ran';
'I eated' instead of 'I ate'.

The future tense that is regularly formed by adding 'will' as in 'I will come', 'I will jump' does not appear in their speech until children develop their concept of future time.

Plurals

The same mistakes will occur as with past tenses, when children need to form the plural of nouns. They learn the regular rule that if they are referring to more than one object, they need to add an 's' such as, 'bed/beds'.

However, this does not work for irregular nouns like mouse (mice), sheep (sheep) and foot (feet). In an attempt to apply the newly learned rule children will often produce the words – 'mouses', 'sheeps' and 'feets'. Gradually they learn the correct form. This is partly achieved by adults responding in the way previously described, that is giving the correct and accepted model of the word, while reinforcing the use of the meaning.

Questions

In the early stages of language development, questions are asked using a rising intonation pattern. For example, 'Me going out?', 'Daddy go work?' Then, children learn that specific question words such as, 'Where? What? Why? When? How?' get both adult attention and information, and they begin to use these words often. Such questions can be a cause of great embarrassment to adults, as they are not always used in the appropriate time and place. This is a great delight to children, often encouraging them to do it again. This is demonstrated in the following example.

On a crowded bus, Lucy (aged three) asks, in a loud voice, about the young girl sitting two seats in front: 'Mummy, why has that lady got pink hair?' Observing the reaction from her mother and everyone else on the bus, Lucy is encouraged to repeat it. The response, reaction as well as the information gained, from using question words means that children will use them frequently.

The third year is often described as the 'why' stage, as this is the age at which children frequently use the word 'why' – not always appropriately.

Word order

Children are learning and absorbing so much new information about their environment and language, that they sometimes get their words in the wrong order. For example, saying sentences like: 'They looked at very funny faces with each other,' instead of, 'They looked at each other with very funny faces.' It is usually when children are trying out new constructions that they make errors. However, even when making errors, children usually succeed in getting their message across correctly.

As children begin to have more to say, they want to talk in longer, more complex sentences. At first they cope with this by linking several short sentences together using the word 'and'. For example, 'And we're going there and teddy and I want dolly and that doll and that one and Rupert Bear.'

Gradually other words, such as 'like', 'but', 'because', 'so', 'or' are used. They enable children to use complex sentences containing more than one idea, linking the ideas together. For example: 'Can we go to the beach, because I want to swim?' or 'I want to go out, but it's raining.'

Conclusion

The normal development of language and communication skills shows a great deal of variation and some children may continue to make grammatical errors until ten years or sometimes even later. The development and expansion of children's language skills continues, going hand in hand with their growing experience.

Further reading

Browne, A. (2001) *Developing Language and Literacy 3–8*, 2nd edn. London: Paul Chapman Publishing.

Coupe O'Kane, J. and Goldbart, J. (1998) *Communication Before Speech*. London: David Fulton Publishers.

Latham, C. and Miles, A. (2001) *Communication, Curriculum and Classroom Practice*. London: David Fulton Publishers.

Chapter 3

Recognising Hearing Problems

Magdalene Moorey and Merle Mahon

This chapter describes what is meant by hearing loss, the effects of a hearing loss on developing speech and language, and considers ways in which problems may be identified and managed.

What is meant by hearing loss?

Hearing ability is usually measured in terms of the quietest sounds that can be detected across a range of frequencies (**pitches** or **tones**). 'Normal' hearing is described as the quietest sounds that can be heard by a large group of young healthy adults. When sounds have to be made louder before a person can detect them then this is described as a raised threshold of hearing or a hearing loss. This can range in severity from mild to profound or total and can affect some frequencies more than others. Some types of hearing loss are temporary, or reversible, others remain throughout life. Different types of problems are more likely to occur at different times in the lifespan.

The causes of hearing loss are many and various. However it is not uncommon for medical notes to state 'aetiology unknown', that is, no one has been able to identify the underlying cause. Some possible causes include:

- inherited disorders;
- damage resulting from infections during pregnancy;
- medication given for potentially life threatening illnesses such as meningitis;
- diseases of the ear.

The hearing mechanism

The hearing mechanism (see Figure 3.1) can be divided into two main parts: the **conductive** system comprising the outer and middle ear, and the **sensory** system of the inner ear.

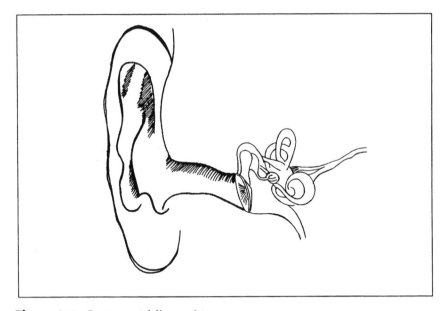

Figure 3.1 Outer, middle and inner ear

The conductive part includes the external ear, the ear canal, ear drum and a chain of tiny bones in the middle ear. Its function is to convey sound energy from the environment to the sensory organ of hearing. It does this by converting sound energy into vibration, which travels along a conductive chain.

The sensory system consists of the organ of hearing, the **cochlea**. This is a coiled, fluid-filled structure that supports millions of tiny sensory 'hair' cells. Vibration moves as a wave through the fluid and the consequent movement in the hair cells creates an electrical signal to be transmitted through the nerve cells to the brain.

It may help to think of the outer and middle ears as part of a mechanical system of levers, drums and moving parts and the inner ear as a nervous system of wires and connections directing an electrical current.

Damage to the hearing mechanism

Damage to the hearing mechanism can occur at any point. The site and extent of any damage will affect the nature and the degree of any hearing loss. Any damage or disruption to the outer and middle ears will reduce the ears' capacity to conduct vibration. This sort of damage is therefore said to give rise to **conductive hearing loss** affecting hearing across the frequency range important for speech (125 Hz – 4,000 Hz). Sound is heard as 'muffled'. Complex sound such as speech may become difficult to hear, with the quieter consonants 'f, s, sh, p' becoming inaudible.

Making speech louder often helps to overcome the hearing loss. There are medical and surgical procedures that can help alleviate the problem. Frequently the conditions that give rise to conductive hearing loss are temporary and may resolve without the need for intervention.

Damage to the inner ear results in a **sensorineural hearing loss**. This can range from mild to profound or total loss in its severity. Hearing for different frequencies can be differently affected: generally, high frequencies are more often affected than low. This gives the result of speech not only sounding quieter but also distorted. A useful comparison is when a battery-operated radio is beginning to run down. Speech becomes fuzzy and indistinct: turning up the volume may make the speech louder but it does not make it easier to understand what is being said.

As sensorineural hearing loss involves damage to nerve cells, there are far fewer medical or surgical interventions that can be employed. Once a nerve cell has been damaged it does not regenerate. However, it is often possible to make use of the hearing that remains through amplification of sound using a hearing aid. Increasingly, **cochlear implants** are being undertaken where there is a severe or profound sensorineural loss. This makes use of an artificially implanted speech processor to replace the function of the damaged cochlea.

Sensorineural hearing loss in young children is still relatively rare in the UK. Studies consistently report an incidence of 1 per 1,000 births. Consequently, a nursery nurse or teacher may meet only one or two deaf infants in their career. In contrast, conductive hearing loss is extremely common in young children: approximately 70 per cent of children have experienced at least one episode of middle ear dysfunction by their third birthday. Although less severe in its impact than sensorineural hearing loss, it is a problem that most carers or educators of young children will encounter.

Middle ear dysfunction

Middle ear dysfunction is a term that is used to describe a range of disturbances to the normal working of the middle ear. It is very common in young children, who may have one or more episodes of middle ear dysfunction in the first years of life.

There are two common causes of this dysfunction:

1. The passage that connects the middle ear to the nose, the **Eustachian tube**, may become blocked. The fresh supply of air needed to keep the middle ear cavity healthy is removed and within weeks the cavity can become full of fluid. In this state the middle ear is significantly less effective in conducting sound to the cochlea. The fluid in the middle ear thickens over time and after a number of weeks may have the consistency of glue, hence the familiar label '**glue ear**'.

2. The middle ear may become infected. If the Eustachian tube is closed off by swelling of membranes or enlarged tonsils or adenoids and there is an infection, pus may collect in the middle ear. This can cause extreme pain and pressure on the ear drum, causing it to tear. This is one of the most common reasons for parents attending casualty departments with an inconsolable and feverish child. Once the drum has burst however, pressure is relieved and the child quietens. While the drum can naturally repair very quickly, repeated tearing will result in a build up of scar tissue and small but permanent changes in hearing levels can remain. If infection is left untreated, life-threatening complications can develop where, in extreme cases, infection passes to the covering of the brain.

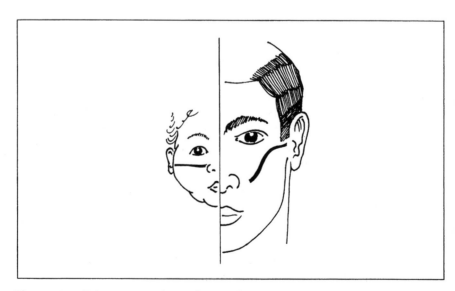

Figure 3.2 Diagram to show the angle of the Eustachian tube in the infant and the adult

The conditions described above are collectively known as **Otitis Media** and are much more common in children than adults. This is because the horizontal angle of the Eustachian tube in children makes it more likely for blockages to occur (see Figure 3.2). It is also thought to be related to children's immature mechanisms for fighting infection. Otitis Media is more common in the winter months and in children with a low birth weight. Certain groups of children are more prone to developing middle ear dysfunction, such as children with Down's Syndrome or a cleft palate.

Treatment of middle ear dysfunction

Treatments for middle ear dysfunction vary widely according to the preferences of ENT surgeons and local hospital policy. The Effective Healthcare Bulletin (1992) on the 'Treatment of persistent glue ear in children' recommended the approach of 'watchful waiting' to identify those children who had a persistent period of substantial hearing impairment. Surgery should only be considered for this group of children if their problems persist through the period of 'watchful waiting'. This approach prevents a surgical procedure being performed on children whose problems clear spontaneously. Subsequent rates of surgery for middle ear dysfunction have reduced significantly ever since.

Treatment with surgery

Guidance on referral practice for children with 'persistent Otitis Media with effusion (glue ear)' was published by the National Institute for Clinical Excellence (NICE) in 2000 (www.nice.org.uk). This clearly states the conditions under which referral – immediate, urgent, soon or routine – should be made and includes:

- suspected serious complications arising from chronic infection;
- suspicion of additional sensorineural hearing loss;
- persistent hearing loss on two occasions at least three months apart;
- speech, language or behavioural difficulty;
- a second disability such as Down's Syndrome;
- frequent acute, infected Otitis Media.

An ENT surgeon may then consider surgery to clean the middle ear and to insert a ventilation tube or **grommet**. This is a tiny, hooked plastic tube that sits across the ear drum acting as a permanently open window. Its function is to allow a free flow of air into the middle ear, particularly when the Eustachian tube is non-functioning. It is not to allow fluid or pus to drain from the ear, as many mistakenly believe. If there is any discharge when grommets are *in situ* this often means the grommets have ceased to be effective or have fallen out spontaneously. Most grommets are designed to fall out without the need for surgical removal. This takes on average six months but can vary from two weeks to two years. Occasionally, where a surgeon has reason to believe that middle ear dysfunction is likely to be a long-term problem, a T-Tube may be fitted. This is a larger grommet, which has to be removed by a surgeon when no longer needed.

Tonsillectomy and/or adenoidectomy may be undertaken, if the tonsils/adenoids are prone to repeated infection or if they are swollen and causing the Eustachian tube to be obstructed.

Treatment with medication

Some doctors will prescribe a course of antibiotics if there is an acute Otitis Media, with or without glue ear. Antibiotics may also be given where there is an enlarged or infected tonsil or adenoid that is thought to be contributing to the Eustachian tube dysfunction.

What to look for in a child with hearing problems

The following points may alert an observant parent, nursery nurse or teacher to the possibility of a hearing loss.

1. The child does not turn when called.
2. Hearing seems to fluctuate from day to day – sometimes the child will respond to speech at normal conversational levels, other times only to a 'shout'. Adults may say 'He hears when he wants to.'
3. The child seems particularly interested and attentive to visual cues, for example watching the speaker's face.
4. The child's behaviour changes noticeably – a normally friendly, settled child becomes aggressive, tearful or withdrawn.
5. The child is distracted easily without one to one attention. In a group he or she may wander off, or be a step behind the other children, watching to see what to do next.
6. The child shows a marked difference in responsiveness in quiet conditions compared to where there is a lot of background noise.

7. Language and speech development may be slowed down or seem to deteriorate after a cold. Speech may be hard to understand and the sentence structures the child uses may be simpler than those used by other children of a similar age.
8. The child may complain of painful or 'funny' ears, or pull at or bang the ears.
9. The child may be turning the TV/video volume up or choose to sit very near to the screen.
10. The child may speak louder or softer than usual.

Middle ear problems and language development

The effect of a permanent, significant hearing loss present from around birth has major implications for spoken language learning. Despite a normal ability to acquire language, the child may have difficulties both in understanding what is said and in being understood. Initially, language may seem to be similar to that expected of a younger child. As the child grows the impact of a hearing loss may be evident in the development of the child's language structure, language use and speech.

The impact of middle ear dysfunction on language development and communication is less clear. A great deal of research has been undertaken to attempt to clarify the relationship. The outcomes can be summarised.

- Approximately half of the children who are referred to speech and language therapists with delayed language development have a significant history of persistent middle ear dysfunction.
- Children with middle ear dysfunction are more likely to have language difficulties when there is a second predisposing factor. This may be a family history of such problems, or birth difficulties.
- The difficulty that arises is delayed language. For the majority of children this delay does not usually persist beyond Key Stage 1. The educational impact is seen in the number of children who have difficulties developing literacy skills following a history of persistent middle ear dysfunction in the early years.

In summary, the impact of middle ear dysfunction would appear to depend on many factors including the severity and persistence of the hearing loss, other factors in the child's history that predispose them to language learning problems, and the personality of the child.

Identifying hearing problems

There are two main ways of identifying hearing problems in children:

1. The use of neonatal or infant screening programmes aimed at picking out children who do not respond to a given test or task in a way expected of the majority of their peers.
2. Picking out those children who by their behaviour in an everyday setting seem to be having difficulty with hearing, listening or communication.

The first method is usually carried out by child-health staff and relies on every child in the target group being covered by the screening programme. The second relies on information from individual child-health surveillance staff as well as concerned parents.

Formal assessment of hearing

In the UK most health authorities carry out a screening test of hearing on children during the first year of life – the **Health Visitor Distraction Test** (HVDT). It is a behavioural test in which a baby has to give an observable indication that the sound has been heard (usually a head turn). It is carried out at seven to eight months when the infant has head and trunk control. The baby is seated on the parent's knee and sounds are presented behind and to the left and right of the baby's head. The baby must turn in response to each sound presented to pass the test. A pass is achieved if the baby responds to low and high frequency tones on the left and right. If necessary, the baby is retested a few weeks later and if there is a repeated fail the baby is referred for diagnostic assessment at an audiology clinic. See McCormick (1993) for a full description of the test; see Davis (1998) for a review of infant screening programmes.

Where a child is known to be at high risk for hearing loss, it is increasingly common for that child to be screened in the first few days of life. Often this is in a hospital or in a special care baby unit. This testing is carried out using one or more 'objective' tests. These are tests where the baby only needs to be still, or asleep, so that the integrity of physical structures or nervous pathways can be assessed. From the results, hearing levels are inferred. It is concluded that a baby does not have a significant hearing loss if the test results show a normal function of the middle ear, and electrical responses occur at a number of points on the auditory nerve pathway.

Research shows that in 1998 25 per cent of deaf children were not identified until after the age of three and a half. A small number of health authorities are now running pilot schemes offering neonatal screening to all infants. It is anticipated that these pilot schemes will be the beginning of universal neonatal hearing screening for the UK.

While this programme of surveillance is available to children born in the UK and similar systems operate in many other countries, children who have moved to the UK during their early years may not have had an early assessment of their hearing. A number of tests are used for older infants and young children. These do not require a knowledge of English and may be carried out by a school nurse or a health visitor.

A child's health records should include the results of any hearing assessments carried out, which will give an indication of whether there has been intermittent hearing loss during the early years. The fact that a child has passed a hearing test is not conclusive proof that they have no hearing difficulties. It should be noted that the nature of most middle ear dysfunction is a cycle of disruption and recovery over a 12 week period. A sensorineural hearing loss affecting one ear may have major implications for listening in a class setting but this may not come to light until a child has failed to make progress in literacy in Key Stage 1 or 2.

Early years provision and hearing problems

Staff in nurseries and Early Years Centres are likely to encounter a number of children at risk for hearing loss. This is partly because of the high incidence of middle ear dysfunction in young children. Also the close proximity of the children makes the spread of infections through the group more likely. The Early Years Centre poses particular challenges for a child with hearing problems.

1. Noise levels where young children gather can be very high. This can become part of the norm and tolerance of high levels of background noise can mean that 'auditory clutter' goes unchecked. For example, if a radio has been left on in a kitchen, or the volume on a computer program is turned up high.
2. Staff–child ratios in most centres means that it may be difficult to be aware of an individual child's day to day fluctuations in hearing levels.
3. There are many factors that affect a child's behaviour (see Chapter 6). Aggression or tearfulness may be wrongly attributed to

difficulties in adjusting to being one of a group of children rather than difficulty of coping with changing hearing levels in a demanding, busy, social environment.

Because language learning is taking place at such a rapid pace in this period, it is important to be aware when a child is having difficulty in hearing the language spoken around them. If there is an awareness of the child's difficulties it is possible to provide an environment where staff can compensate for this difficulty in the way in which interaction, learning and play is managed.

What to do if a hearing loss is suspected

If a hearing loss is suspected there are a number of courses of action.

1. If a child's behaviour suggests that they may not be hearing well, ask the parents whether the child completed and passed infant hearing tests.
2. If these were failed and there are concerns, encourage the parent to seek further testing via the GP.
3. Mention your concerns to the local child-health staff when they visit the early years provision.
4. Follow this up with enquiries regarding the results of any hearing assessments. A copy of the report will often be sent to a school or Early Years Centre.

Ways of helping a child with a hearing loss

For a child with middle ear dysfunction the behaviour of adults is one of the most important factors in coping well with this intermittent condition. There are many positive ways in which early years carers and teachers can help a child with hearing loss, whether permanent or fluctuating.

1. Spend some time listening to the noise in the playrooms and classrooms. Is it all necessary? Can any be removed? Can quieter areas with soft coverings be set up? Can the window be closed for story time?
2. Try to ensure that a child with known or suspected hearing loss is placed towards the front of a group for group sessions – but not so

near that it is hard to see the face of the speaker. Use horseshoe seating patterns rather than irregular rows so that children can see who is talking rather than having their back to the speaker.

3. Try to arrange the day's activities so that each child has some experience of listening in a small group rather than only free play or large group activities.

4. Maintain good lighting in the room, avoiding sitting with your back to a window – your face will be in shadow.

5. It is essential to gain eye contact before beginning to talk to the child. Call their name first and pause until they look up, or use a phrase such as 'Are you ready [name]?'

6. Try to include activities that require listening to speech and non-speech, for example marching to a drum, clapping when you hear your 'word' or name.

7. Try some listening games at quieter levels so that the child learns to use their hearing.

8. Ask a visiting speech and language therapist for some activity ideas for listening tasks and group games.

9. Share information about a child's hearing levels so that all adults can help to support the child and can also understand the child's behaviour.

10. If a child has been prescribed medication such as nose drops, where it is Centre policy to administer these on behalf of parents, staff should ask for instructions and/or a demonstration. Nose drops wrongly used will be ineffective in dealing with congestion.

Further reading

www.deafnessatbirth.org.uk
This is an excellent web site for all those working with young children with hearing impairment. It includes a summary of language development, hearing testing and educational approaches.

www.ndcs.org.uk
This is the parent-friendly web site of the National Deaf Children's Society. It gives basic information on hearing impairment, hearing aids and signing. There is a section on toys and books for deaf children with names of suppliers.

www.unhs.org.uk
This is the web site of the Universal Neonatal Hearing Screening Programme.

www.nice.org.uk
This is the web site for the National Institute for Clinical Excellence, which publishes all agreed national guidelines on best practice in medicine and health care.

Chapter 4

How to Recognise Speech and Language Problems

Rosemarie MorganBarry and Jannet A. Wright

The normal pattern of speech and language development was outlined and the many varied aspects of human communication were described in Chapter 2. When the complexity of the speech and language system is considered, it is amazing that the majority of children manage to enter school with communication skills that enable them to cope with the demands of school life. Even if some of these children were slow to acquire language initially, they will usually have 'caught up' in the preschool years. There are, however, other children whose poor speech and language skills are a cause of anxiety to their parents and to the professionals who care for them, both before and after school entry.

This chapter is concerned with the early recognition of children whose speech and language is slow to develop. Behaviour patterns may be an indication that a child is having problems learning language. It is these behaviours that will be described. This should help professionals caring for such children to be aware of possible speech-language problems and to ask for specialist help for the child as early as possible.

There are two important questions to be considered concerning speech and language in children.

1. How well do children understand the language heard around them?
2. How well can children use speech and language so that other people know what they are saying?

When reading about speech and language delay, 'understanding' is frequently referred to as **reception** or **comprehension** of language, and the output that enables a child to be understood as the **expression** of language (see Chapter 2). Comprehension and expression will be considered in turn, with guidelines and a checklist to highlight possible problems in learning language.

Comprehension

Some children have difficulty understanding what is said to them. This may be because they have problems with hearing (see Chapter 3), or because they are learning English as an additional language, having previously used a different language at home (for example, Bengali, Cantonese, Turkish). However, even without hearing difficulties, or learning English as an additional language, some children are slow in learning to talk, and their understanding is not as good as might be expected for their age.

Children who have problems in understanding are often helped by the 'clues' given to them by adult speakers. These clues may include pointing, gesture and facial expression. In addition, the situation within the home/nursery or school may provide clues for such a child. For example, the instruction: 'Put your coat on, Joshua,' may be accompanied by pointing to the coat-rack, or even holding out the coat. Similarly, questions may be asked, or instructions given, relating to various activities, when the objects being talked about are in front of, or near to the child. For example:

- 'Find the red engine Matthew.'
- 'Emma, where are the scissors?'
- 'Are you going to put some yellow paint on your picture?'
- 'What are you doing to teddy, Simon?'

The same may happen with general instructions, such as those given below, which are all part of the routine of the day, and which most children quickly learn, without needing to understand the individual words. For example:

- 'It's tidy-up time.'
- 'Wash your hands for dinner.'
- 'Come and sit down for story-time.'

Adults, when talking to children, are for the most part unaware of how much help is provided by these 'clues'; they occur naturally and without our thinking about them too much. Try giving someone directions about a route they have to follow, without using your hands.

These clues, gestures and facial expressions can be useful; think about how much you can guess about what's going on when you visit a country where you don't know a word of the language. Children with poor understanding are in just that situation; they rely on these additional clues to help them make sense of what is going on around them.

However, the use of these clues makes it difficult for us to know exactly how much speech and language a child understands. Two teachers were heard to make these observations about the same boy:

'He understands everything that's going on.'
'He doesn't understand a word I say.'

These comments seem to be in total disagreement, but, in fact, both may be true. The boy probably could understand everything that was going on, by watching for the 'clues'; or, it may be that the situation was very familiar to him; but he may not have understood much of what the second teacher actually said. Thus, if unexpectedly asked a question such as, 'Have you got a pet at home, Ben?' it might well have met with nothing more than a blank stare from Ben.

Children with poor understanding can work extremely hard to try and follow instructions. One way they may help themselves may be to watch other children and copy them. In the classroom this may mean that they are last to start an activity or follow an instruction. They may attend to, or hear, only the last word, or words, in a sentence and appear to ignore part of what was said.

In order to establish how much spoken language a child is actually understanding, it is necessary to try and cut out all these additional, helpful clues, and to assess the child's ability to comprehend, using words alone.

When children are learning to talk it is quite common for them to repeat what they have just heard. This is part of learning, and is to be encouraged. However, a child who frequently 'echoes' what was said, and who constantly repeats what adults or children are saying, may have a serious comprehension problem as illustrated below:

Teacher: 'Is it your birthday today?'
Child: 'Birthday.'
Teacher: 'Yes, you're four today!'
Child: 'Four today.'
Teacher: 'Did you have many presents?'
Child: 'Many presents.'

What to look for
- The child who is slow to learn the class routine.
- The child who watches and copies others.
- The child with poor attention at story-time.
- The child who 'echoes'.

- The child who often makes an inappropriate response to questions and instructions.

These behaviours could also indicate learning difficulties and/or lack of confidence, and need to be investigated in more detail.

How to check
- Give simple instructions, without clues, and note the child's response.
- Ask the occasional question, 'out of the blue'.
- Give more complex directions, and possibly unexpected instructions and note exactly what the child does, for example: 'Go to the cupboard and get a piece of blue paper'; or 'Put a Lego brick on the desk before you go outside.'

What to do
- Ask for the child's hearing to be checked (see Chapter 3).
- Ask about language(s) spoken at home.
- Refer to a speech and language therapist.
- Check the child has understood an instruction by asking them to repeat what you have just said.
- Watch closely to see if the child's response is appropriate for your instructions.
- Use short, simple instructions.
- Make use of everyday gesture to aid understanding.

Expression

There are a number of important aspects of speech and language, all of which are necessary in order to be understood when talking to other people. These are:

- the sounds (**articulation**), which make up
- the words (**vocabulary**) which must be in
- the right order (**syntax**) and
- appropriate to the situation (**pragmatics**).

If any of these areas are slow to develop, then communication can break down. The child will not be able to get the message across and this can become a serious problem as the child gets older.

Each of these areas will be considered in turn.

Articulation

This area is concerned with a child's mastery of the sounds of the language (see Chapter 2). Young children take time, literally, to get their tongues round the sounds of the language, and many – but not all – children practise these sounds in the babbling stage of infancy as described in Chapter 2. Some sounds are easier to make than others:

/m/ as in mummy, more
/n/ as in nana, no
/b/ as in baby, bye
/d/ as in daddy.

These are all quite straightforward and are usually the first sounds a child produces.

Slightly more difficult sounds are:

/k/ (written also as 'c') as in kitten, car
/g/ as in go

while the following sounds are all quite difficult:

/f/ as in finger
/v/ as in van
/s/ as in sun, sea
/ch/ as in chip
/r/ as in rabbit
/sh/ as in shoe, ship, sugar.

Words and phrases in which a number of these more difficult sounds occur together require the tongue and lips to perform some quite difficult gymnastics. In a word like 'nana', there are only two sounds, which are repeated, and the tongue does not have a great deal to do, but in a phrase such as 'fish and chips', there are nine different sounds:

'f–i–sh – a–n – ch–i–p–s' = Nine sounds

(when talking quickly you rarely say/hear the 'd' at the end of 'and'). All of this involves the tongue in some tricky manoeuvres. Try saying 'fish and chips' slowly to yourself and think about how you do it.

It is therefore not at all uncommon, or surprising, to hear young children producing common immaturities such as:

'wabbit' for rabbit
'tip' for chip
'pi' or 'pit' for fish.

Sometimes, they get some of the sounds right but put them in the wrong place. For example, Ella (aged three years) could say:

'tis an fips' (fish and chips).

She managed the difficult /s/ and /f/ sounds, but got them in the wrong order. Other examples of getting sounds the wrong way round in a word are:

'efalant' elephant
'tefalone' telephone
'hostipul' hospital.

Other common immaturities include:

'tar' car
'dot' got

and words in which the tongue comes forward in a lisp as in:

'thun' sun
'thock' sock.

Sometimes children miss the /s/ at the beginning of some words, for example:

'poon' spoon
'tar' star
'carf' scarf.

This is because the second sound of the word is a **consonant** and the tongue and lips have some difficult manoeuvres to make. It is easier to say words in which a **vowel** follows a consonant, as in:

'c a r' 's a y' 't oo l' 'n ai l'

than to say words where two consonants occur next to each other, as in:

'sc a r' 'st a y' 'st oo l' 'sn ai l'

especially when one of the two consonants in the consonant cluster is the difficult /s/ sound.

By the time children near their fourth birthday, many of the immature pronunciations should have disappeared.

Phonology

This is related to articulation and the speech sounds of language. The word 'phonology' is used by speech and language therapists to refer to the way in which individual sounds are put together to make words, such that changing a sound within a word will make a change in meaning. For example, children learn quite early on that there is a difference between

'*p*ear' and '*b*ear'
'*c*at' and '*h*at'
'mou*th*' and 'mou*se*'
'p*u*ppy' and 'p*o*ppy'
'Da*nn*y' and 'Da*dd*y'
'dog' and 'dog*s*'

By changing (or adding) one sound in each of these pairs of words (known as **minimal pairs**) there is a resultant change of meaning.

Most children learn how the sound system of the language works, but how they do this is one of the wonders of child language development. Nobody teaches them how to recognise that different sounds make different meanings; they learn the rules of phonology in much the same way as they work out for themselves the rules of grammar (see Chapter 2). The context in which the words are used helps to make the meaning clear, although this may not always work.

The examples of the pronunciations given earlier showed that, although young children may be aware of how sounds in a language work together to make words and change meaning, they do not in the early years have the necessary ability to put their lips and tongues around the sounds to give the complete adult pronunciation.

Other children may have different problems. Children with hearing problems (see Chapter 3) have difficulty hearing the small differences that carry meaning; therefore they may be unable to produce them accurately, thus making their speech hard to understand. Some children whose hearing for everyday sounds seems adequate may have particular difficulty in distinguishing the small differences between sounds: /p/ and /b/; /f/ and /v/. Also sounds like 'tr' as in '*tr*ain' and 'ch' as in '*ch*ain' may sound very alike unless you listen closely. Speech and language therapists, therefore, use tests containing sets of minimal pairs of words (MorganBarry 1988) to check how well children hear and discriminate the differences between them.

Some children, although able to discriminate speech sounds, nonetheless use only a few sounds to do the work of many.

Gary, aged three years nine months, used the /g/ sound most of the time. For example he would say:

'I wan go geep bu egun maging goig.'
[I want (to) go (to) sleep but everyone (is) making (a) noise.]

He uses the /g/ sound instead of /sl/ in 'sleep', /v/ in 'everyone', /k/ in 'making' and /z/ at the end of 'noise'. He also missed some words out – see **syntax** below.

All this makes his speech very hard to understand. His mother could understand him, but other family members and friends often had to ask for a translation. This is because his mother has got used to Gary's style of pronunciation. People who are in daily contact with such children may become familiar with their unusual speech. This does not necessarily mean that the children are speaking more clearly, but that the listener has become more used to their speech patterns.

These speech patterns are called 'phonological systems'; a child such as Gary may have his own phonological system which changes and develops as he gradually acquires more sounds, and as he learns to fit these sounds together to match the adult phonological system of the language. Not all children manage this task; they are then described as having a 'phonological disorder'.

Phonological disorders may occur in different ways. For example, there are children who may not have all of the sounds, like Stacey, aged four, who said:

'Dit my pable, I'm puttin tup om it.'
[This (is) my table, I'm putting cup(s) on it.]

Other children, however, may have most, or all, of the sounds, but use them so variably that they remain unintelligible. If, in addition, they omit certain sounds, the result is a problem for the listener. This sentence from Michelle, age seven, is an example:

'You dot one bat tipey tot an one bap potty pok.'
['You've got one black stripey sock and one black spotty sock.']

It is important to remember that while many children grow out of early speech difficulties, some need help before they get to school, where teachers and other children expect them to be able to communicate clearly. Simple problems like lisping may sort themselves out, but parents, teachers and nursery staff need to be alert to children like Gary and Stacey, who have more complex problems. Some children who have speech difficulties that are complex, severe or unusual may later experience difficulty with reading, writing and spelling (Simpson 2001).

What to look for
- The child who cannot be understood by adults outside the family.
- The child who sounds 'muddled'.

- The child who appears to have only a few sounds.
- The child who says the same word differently at different times.

How to check
- Look at a book or pictures with a child in a quiet corner and listen to him/her. It is important to listen carefully because it is easy to think the child has said a word correctly when you have understood what she or he has said.
- Name pictures for the child and encourage him/her to imitate you – notice how each word is said.

What to do
- Ask for the child's hearing to be checked.
- Ask whether family and friends have commented on the child's speech.
- Refer to the speech and language therapist.
- Do not mimic the child to their face.
- Say the word correctly in a sentence following their incorrect attempt, but do not repeat the incorrect pronunciation to the child.

Vocabulary

Some children do not have the words or vocabulary which one might expect for their age. For example, Daniel, aged six years, was looking at a book with his mother.

Mother: 'Oh look, there's a . . . '
Daniel: 'That.'
Mother: 'Yes, it's a car.'
Daniel: 'Car.'
Mother: 'They're going on the . . . '
Daniel: 'That.'
Mother: 'Yes, the road.'

When talking about the pictures, Daniel does not appear to have the vocabulary to describe the picture. He should have been able to do this by the age of four years when one would expect a child to name objects that they can see in a picture, and talk about some of the actions.

Adults await children's first words with eager anticipation and often record them in a book. When children are first learning to talk their parents can easily remember the words they can say. But, very quickly it becomes impossible to keep track as children's vocabulary grows at such a rapid rate.

An activity such as the one Daniel is doing, naming pictures in a book, is often more appropriate with children in the first two to three years of life. It provides them with the opportunity to learn and practise new words. This is why they frequently choose the same book for adults to read to them, so that they have a chance to practise or rehearse new vocabulary. By the time they are Daniel's age they are more interested in listening to and retelling a story.

A child who appears to have difficulty learning new words, or remembering words, could have a language delay. Their speech may sound clear and their sentence structures appear appropriate for what they want to say, but their vocabulary may not be increasing in the way one would expect.

What to look for
- A child who finds it hard to remember the names of objects and the names of other children in the class.
- A child who has trouble learning new words.
- A child who uses 'this'/'that' a great deal without naming items/ objects.
- A child who is not always fluent (see Chapter 5).

How to check
- Choose an unfamiliar book or toy to look at with the child. After talking about a few of the pictures or items see if the child can tell you what they are. Try again the next day, and again the day after.
- If a child cannot name an object see if he/she can tell you what it is used for.

What to do
- Choose a topic such as fruit, transport or animals and draw the child's attention to certain words during a week. See if they remember them in two weeks' time.
- Find out if remembering or learning new words is a problem in other situations, for example, playschool, nursery, school or with grandparents.
- Ask the speech and language therapist to see the child.
- See Chapters 8 and 9.

Syntax

Sam, aged four years, explained how his father was carrying out some do-it-yourself.

'My dad out went hammer, got hammer wood got down.'
Sam manages to get his message across, but the words are not in the order we would expect. It sounds strange. In English words are put in a certain order in a sentence, this is the grammar or syntax of the language. If children have difficulties in this area their sentences may be very short in length or they may sound 'odd' because the order is incorrect. Sometimes children talk using the correct sounds, and, as the adult can understand what they are saying, it is easy to ignore the fact that the words are not in the right order. The following sentence shows this.

Laura (aged five years): 'Mummy, ice-cream me have?'
Mother: 'Later, when we go to the shops.'
Laura's mother understands that Laura is asking for an ice-cream, she is used to Laura's syntax, but to a stranger this would sound unusual.

It is more common for children to have both poor articulation and syntax, which makes it very difficult for the listener to understand their speech. Remember the examples of Gary and Stacey given earlier in this chapter.

Telegrammatic speech

Sometimes when listening to a very young child or an older child who has difficulty with syntax the listener is aware that the child's speech sounds rather like a verbal telegram. This type of speech in fact has been called telegrammatic speech, and you can see why if you read the examples below:

'Me go school now,' instead of: 'I go to school now.'
'Daddy go work car,' instead of: 'Daddy goes to work in the car.'

In these examples the children retain the words that carry the information in the sentence. It does sound like a telegram.

However, if children have a problem with syntax, they are unlikely to leave out words from choice, it is more likely that they cannot cope with a longer utterance, or that they have failed to learn the linking words.

The linking words in the phrases above include 'to', 'in', 'the'. If a child is two years old the omission of these linking words would not cause concern. At this age children string together the important words so that when telling an adult what they intend to do, 'Me go garden' is perfectly acceptable. However, if a child is still doing this at four years old, then there would be cause for concern because at this age you would expect to hear, 'I want to go in the garden.'

The following example indicates a severe problem in a five-year-old boy, describing an outing with his parents.

'Mummy, Daddy, me went car, long time, shops, ice-cream new shirt.'

This child gets his message across, but the listener has to do a lot of work in order to understand that he meant:

- Mummy, Daddy and child went in the car;
- it was a long way to town;
- the child had an ice-cream in a restaurant;
- a new shirt was bought for the child.

If you suspect a child is having problems with syntax, the following suggestions may help.

What to look for
- A child missing words out of a sentence.
- A child who gets words in the wrong order in a sentence.
- A child whose speech sounds a bit like a telegram.

How to check
- Listen carefully to children when they are telling a story, or talking about something they have just done.
- Note down exactly what they say, do not add in any extra words.
- Look at your notes: have they left any words out? Or are any of the words in an order that surprises you?

What to do
- Provide the correct, full-length version of the child's sentence after they have spoken to you, but do not expect them to repeat it (see 'Modelling' in Chapter 2).
- Ask the speech and language therapist to see the child.
- Do not mimic the child's speech.

Children who have problems, or who are delayed in learning to talk, often have all these types of difficulty at the same time: difficulties with sounds, with vocabulary, with syntax. These are the children who are 'reluctant communicators', who say little, often only speaking one or two words at a time; who point and use gesture to help them 'ask' for what they want, and who are unwilling to talk with people they do not know well.

Pragmatics

Conversation is not just two people talking, each saying something in turn; what they say should be linked in some way. If it is not linked, it is like a crossed line on the telephone with two unconnected conversations going on.

A normal conversation with a four-year-old would go something like this:

Samantha (aged four years): 'I got new shoes.'
Teacher: 'Did you? How nice.'
Samantha: 'Yes, they're red.'
Teacher: 'Where did you get them?'
Samantha: 'My mum and me went to the shop.'

Now look at this conversation between Tracy, aged five years, and her teacher:

Tracy: 'I got new shoes.'
Teacher: 'Did you? How nice.'
Tracy: 'I got new shoes.'
Teacher: 'I know, you just told me.'
Tracy: 'I'm doing painting now.'

This conversation is not as successful as the one with Samantha and it is typical of Tracy's conversations with adults and children. Tracy knows how to attract adult attention, but cannot maintain the conversation. A successful continuation of this exchange would probably have involved Tracy pointing to the shoes and getting the adult to look at them, instead of repeating her first statement.

Pragmatics refers to the use of language, how we choose an appropriate way of talking, depending on the situation we find ourselves in. You might ask a child to shut the door by saying:

'Shut the door please, Timmy.'

To an adult you might say any of these:

'Could you shut the door?'
'Would you mind shutting the door?'
'Do you want to shut the door?'

You probably use a different style of speech to adults you know well, such as family members and friends, than to those you are meeting for the first time. Children usually learn these differences quite unconsciously, but some children have to be taught appropriate use of language.

When talking to children who have difficulty in the area of pragmatics, a number of features may be apparent. They may have particular difficulty in linking their responses to the other speaker's comments. For example, when doing some craft work at school, the teacher said, 'Look, the paper has stuck to the table.' The response from the child was, 'We've got yellow tables like this at home.'

Children with such difficulties are poor at taking turns in a conversation, so they constantly interrupt and their comments are not related. It is normal for young children to interrupt if they see or hear something novel such as a fire engine going by, but, by school entry, constant interruptions and inappropriate comments may signal a problem. Such children may also have difficulty taking turns in games in the classroom or any group activities.

They may not know how to attract the adult's attention when starting a conversation. Children without any problems may call out to the adult passing by, or say, 'Guess what!' 'Look,' or 'See this,' or they may pull an adult's sleeve. A child who finds it difficult, or is unable to attract adult attention, may start talking without looking at the adult. It may sound as if they are talking to themselves. The adult eventually becomes aware that the child is talking to them and that a response is needed.

They may not know how to talk about a person or object that is not present. Such children assume that the listener knows what they are referring to. To the listener it may feel like they are coming into a conversation half way through.

Such children can have difficulty linking topics in a conversation and if the conversation breaks down they do not know how to start it up again or 'repair' it.

What to look for
- A child who has problems taking turns in a conversation.
- A child whose conversation continually moves from one topic to the next, fairly rapidly, for no reason.
- A child who cannot switch topics and goes on and on about a subject.
- A classroom environment that may be adding to the child's problems. The adult's language may be too complex, there may not be enough time for the child to understand what is said to them and for them to respond.

How to check
- Listen to the child in conversation with another adult.
- Listen to the child in conversation with another child, and with a group of children.
- Watch how the child gets adult attention.

- Note if the child is able to take turns in the conversation.
- Look at the complexity of the adult's language. This may be causing a breakdown in communication, because the child does not understand what the adult is saying.

What to do
- This is a very complex area of communication to help. It is therefore best to ask a speech and language therapist to see the child.

Summary

This chapter outlines some of the reasons why it can be hard to identify a child who has difficulty understanding speech and language.

Examples are given of problems that can occur with articulation, vocabulary, syntax and pragmatics.

It is important to remember that, as listeners, we are very good at interpreting what we hear people say to us. When talking with children, the most important aspect is listening to what they say, so we can respond appropriately. But, in order to watch out for potential difficulties, we also have to learn to listen to how they say it.

Adults who work with children are in the frontline of identifying speech and language problems. It is often the child's behaviour, such as temper tantrums and/or withdrawal from speech situations, that causes adults to suspect a delay in development.

Further reading

Shields, J. (2001) 'Working with children with comprehension difficulties', in Kersner, M. and Wright, J. A. (eds) *Speech and Language Therapy: The decision-making process when working with children*, 140–50. London: David Fulton Publishers.

Simpson, S. (2001) 'Working with children with written language difficulties', in Kersner, M. and Wright, J. A. (eds) *Speech and Language Therapy: The decision-making process when working with children*, 201–14. London: David Fulton Publishers.

Wood, J. (2001) 'Working with children with language delay and specific language impairment (SLI)' in Kersner, M. and Wright, J. A. (eds) *Speech and Language Therapy: The decision-making process when working with children*, 151–62. London: David Fulton Publishers.

Chapter 5

Stammering in Young Children

Renée Byrne

'Don't worry, he'll grow out of it.' This advice may be given to parents of children who are starting to stammer (Christie 2000). Some children do grow out of it, but some do not. Equally, some parents stop worrying, and some do not. Parents may feel anxiety that is out of all proportion to the child's speech problem because they feel helpless and guilty and do not know what to do.

This chapter explains what is happening when children stammer, and advice is offered about what may be done to help the child at home, in the nursery or at school. Questions that speech and language therapists are frequently asked will be addressed, and suggestions will be made about what to do and what not to do when a child's speech is not fluent.

Stammering, stuttering and disfluency

There is no difference between stammering and stuttering – the term used is largely a matter of choice.

The word 'disfluent' just means not fluent. All of us are disfluent at times, especially when tired, excited or confused about what we are trying to say; we all hesitate when speaking, insert 'mmm' and 'er', repeat sounds and words. We get mixed up about what we want to say, or cannot choose sufficiently quickly between two words and so become stuck for a moment. This behaviour is called 'normal disfluency' (Van Riper 1982) and it is not stammering because, whereas *all stammering is disfluent, not all disfluency is stammering.*

If adults have episodes of disfluency in their speech, is it any wonder that the vast majority of children, before the age of five, go through a period of normal disfluency? Some children have little difficulty learning the complex skills required for the acquisition of speech and language (as discussed in Chapter 2); but for others, learning to speak is quite a struggle.

Just as children do not crawl across the floor at one moment and then immediately stand up and walk down the stairs without constantly falling, picking themselves up and trying again, so most children do not acquire speech and language without experiencing some difficulties. They stumble in their speech just as they stumble when learning to walk; they hesitate, repeat sounds, words and phrases, pause and try again. This behaviour occurs in most young children when they are learning to talk and it is called normal disfluency as referred to above. However, although the majority of children go through a period of normal disfluency, only 4 to 5 per cent show signs of the early stages of stammering (Andrews and Harris 1964).

What are the signs of early stammering?

Repetitions

- of sounds, for example, m . . . m . . . m . . . mummy;
- of syllables, for example, din . . . din . . . dinner;
- of words, for example, more . . . more . . . more drink,
- of phrases, for example, can I have, can I have?

Sound and syllable repetitions are associated more typically with stammering than are word and phrase repetitions (Adams 1977).

However, repetitions are heard in all children, and it is only when they are heard frequently that they may be considered to be a mild sign of stammering.

Prolongations

Prolongations is 'holding on to sounds' such as 'r', 'l', 's', 'sh', 'f', as in: ffffffffffather or lllllllittle.

The prolongation of sounds is heard less commonly in fluent speech than repetitions. When prolongations are heard in a child's speech they do not necessarily indicate that the child is stammering. They must be considered in the context of the whole of the child's speech pattern before they can be thought of as an early warning sign of stammering.

Blocks

Blocks are sometimes described as 'getting stuck'. In this situation speech actually stops. This speech behaviour may cause distress to parents and, sometimes, momentary discomfort to the child. It is often an early sign of stammering. However, a speech and language therapist would consider many other features of the child and his/her speech before making a diagnosis of 'stammering'.

Struggle, tension and fear

If children become aware of their speech difficulties, they may struggle and become tense in order to release themselves from the unpleasant sensations of the stammer. Struggle, tension and fear indicate the beginning of true stammering, and help is required.

Avoidance

If children feel unhappy about their speech, then they may try to use tricks and devices to avoid and hide the stammer from other people. They may avoid certain words by not using them or changing them for others, for example saying 'small' instead of 'little', or 'magic' instead of 'good'. They may avoid talking to certain people, particularly those in authority. When in class, they may avoid speaking by not answering questions, or not asking for things they need such as another piece of paper. Unfortunately, the more they try to avoid and hide, the more fearful they may become and so the stammer tends to get worse. At the same time, the stammer may remain less noticeable to others, because it is largely hidden. Avoidance behaviour is a true sign of stammering because it is not a behaviour found in fluent people and it indicates that the child is acutely aware of a difficulty while speaking.

Repetitions, prolongations and blocks are heard in the speech of most young children, and it is only when they occur too frequently or with great severity that they may indicate the first, mild signs of stammering.

Struggle, tension, fear and avoidance tend to mean that the child is stammering.

What is the difference between normal disfluency and early stammering?

There are several tests and assessments which may be used by speech and language therapists in order to assess disfluent children, for example 'Continuum of Disfluent Speech Behaviours' (Gregory and Hill 1993); 'Stuttering Prediction Instrument for Young Children' (Riley 1981); 'A Component Model for Treating Stuttering in Children' (Riley and Riley

1984); and 'A Chronicity Prediction Checklist' (Cooper and Cooper 1985). Most of these examine three important areas to be discussed with parents or carers:

- The history of the child and the family. Questions will be asked about other members of the family who may stammer, about when the child began saying words, when the disfluency was first noticed, and whether the child's speech is getting better or worse.
- Attitudes, such as how the parents feel about their child's speech, and whether the child reacts to being disfluent.
- The speech of the child, including the frequency and duration of episodes of disfluency, as well as the child's language and articulatory skills.

The difference between normal disfluency and early stammering may not always be clear but, in this context, it is important to note that the therapist is concerned with the general speech and communicative skills of the child, and not solely with the disfluent aspects.

General speech

Research shows that many children who are thought to be stammering have difficulty in learning the words to express themselves (Murray and Reed 1977) or they may be slow in mastering the fine, coordinating muscular movements needed to articulate the sounds of speech (Conture and Caruso 1987). As adults, we are aware that when we cannot think of the right word to use, or when we do not know how to pronounce a word, we will hesitate and pause. It becomes obvious that a child who has a language delay or an articulatory difficulty is at risk of becoming disfluent.

Jim for example is a very excited three and a half-year-old. He is at the zoo for the first time, where he sees an elephant. He desperately wants to tell his mother about this huge, grey elephant, but he does not have the language to express the concept of 'huge', nor the articulatory competence to say a word like elephant. So, you may well hear Jim saying, 'Mum . . . Mum . . . Mummy, look at the . . . the . . . the big . . . big mum . . . mmm the . . . the thing.'

Jim may be thought to be stammering, and could be sent to a speech and language therapist. However, as he is very young, he may be normally disfluent, or he could have a language and/or articulation delay. The speech and language therapist will use specifically designed speech and language tests and assessments in order to differentiate between early stammering and some other speech problem.

If the speech and language therapist finds that Jim has begun to stammer then the question often asked is: 'Why does he stammer?' There is no simple answer. There is rarely a single reason. A stammer is usually the result of a combination of different factors (Rustin *et al.* 1996). Research by Yairi and Ambrose (1999) defines a number of risk factors that incline a child to develop a persistent stammer.

The speech and language therapist will carry out an assessment in order to establish whether the child is at risk for persistent stammering or is going through a stage of normal disfluency. Family history, attitudes and general speech competence have previously been mentioned and, within these areas, there are specific issues, which may be of special significance:

- *High self-expectations* – Some children try to be perfect, and tend to blame themselves for all sorts of everyday problems that arise at home or at school.
- *Articulatory problems* – Some children have difficulty in managing the fine muscular movements required to produce accurate sounds and syllables.
- *Disruptive communication environment* – Children's speech may be disturbed by the attitudes and behaviour of people in their environment, especially if these are people with whom they need to communicate.
- *Unrealistic parental expectations* – The standards of general behaviour, and of speech, which the parents expect may be too high for the child to attain (Starkweather and Gottwald 1990).

When should a disfluent child be referred to a speech and language therapist?

Children should be referred to a speech and language therapist as soon as the parent, nursery nurse, teacher or other significant adult becomes concerned about their speech over a period of time. If the adult is specifically concerned about the child's disfluency, then research shows that the earlier the child is referred, the greater are the chances of permanent fluency (Meyers and Woodford 1992; Riley and Riley 1984). Children as young as two to two and a half years old are now regularly referred to the speech and language therapist. If this seems young to you, then it is important to understand the therapist's role with children within this age group. Initially, the most important role is one of deciding whether the child is showing signs of early stammering, has some other speech and language problem, or is going through a normal stage of speech development. With very young children, the therapist will make an assessment through discussion with parents and a play session with the child so that there is no raising of awareness and no pressure. The findings can then be discussed with the parents and reassurance can be given if there is no problem or, if a difficulty is found, then suitable therapy or help will be suggested.

If it is thought that there is a risk for long-term stammering, then a management programme will be offered. There are a wide range of programmes described in the literature from which the therapist will choose the most suitable depending on the severity of the stammer, the child's reaction to the stammer and the parents' feelings about the stammer. It should be mentioned that, even if a young child's stammer is quite severe, he/she may not continue to stammer.

There are some general 'Dos' and 'Don'ts' about ways in which young disfluent children may be helped (see below), but the therapist will suggest management strategies specific to that child and his/her environment. Indirect work with the parents or carers, or direct work with the child is a possibility and, whichever route is chosen, fluency will be enhanced and disfluency minimised.

The therapist will always take care not to create anxiety about disfluency or stammering where none exists. Some parents do not send their child for speech and language therapy because they fear that the therapist will mention the word 'stammer' and that this will make matters worse. They may think that, if speech is not mentioned, the child will not become anxious and may well 'grow out' of the stammer. This belief is quite wrong. A large proportion of adults who stammer talk about their feelings of isolation when, as children, they were well aware of their difficulty, but could find no one to talk to about it. Those who tried were often told that there was nothing wrong with their speech or that they should not worry. They did worry, but stopped telling anyone.

Therapists do not create anxiety nor do they talk about 'stammering' if the child is unaware. Conversely, they do not participate in a 'conspiracy of silence' that so often surrounds the child who stammers and which, in itself, creates anxiety. If children are worried about their speech, then they will welcome some help and a chance to talk.

What is the difference between early stammering and stammering in the older child or adult?

Stammering is essentially a developmental problem and so grows and changes over time. Stammering has been compared to an iceberg

(Sheehan 1970). A part of the iceberg can be clearly seen above the surface of the water; but another part is hidden beneath the surface of the water. It is this part which may cause most of the problems.

Although hidden, the part that is below the surface is an integral part of the whole iceberg. Like an iceberg, stammering in teenagers and adults has an outward part and a hidden portion. Everything above the surface is the speech symptoms which can be seen and heard; everything below the surface is the feelings and attitudes which are hidden inside the person, and not seen by other people. It is essential that the part below the surface, although hidden, is considered, together with the speech symptoms, when working with the child.

The amount showing above the surface at any one time can change, because the stammer and the feelings associated with it are not constant in any one person; they change according to circumstances.

Figure 5.1 illustrates the situation found in small children, usually below the age of five years, but sometimes as late as 11 to 12 years. Theirs is mainly a speech problem. Young children often attach little importance to their stammer or lack of fluency; they may not be aware that there is anything wrong. If they are aware, they may not be concerned or worried because speech is not an issue for them. The speech problem is mostly of a simple nature because it is above the surface and out in the open.

Figure 5.2 illustrates the situation for an older child, teenager or adult. The speech symptoms, that is, the stammer on the surface, may have increased in frequency and/or severity but, more importantly, the hidden area beneath the surface is now much more significant.

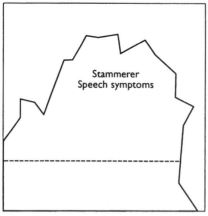

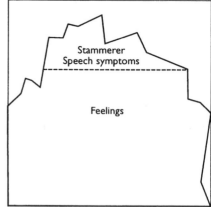

Figure 5.1 Iceberg A, the young child

Figure 5.2 Iceberg B, the older child or adult

For example, Liz is 16 years old. She has experienced considerable social displeasure and negative reactions to her stammering. She has been told that she stammers, asked to take a deep breath and try again. She has been teased and has experienced difficulty in answering to her name in class and in reading aloud. Over a period of time, all these experiences have made her realise that stammering is not the best thing that could have happened to her!

She may now have developed feelings of worry, anxiety, embarrassment or anger, but these feelings will be hidden inside her – the submerged part of the iceberg. How this affects her will depend on her personality, the help she was given in the early years and the support on which she can rely. However, the more afraid, angry or depressed she becomes, the more she is likely to stammer, so that she is caught in a vicious circle.

Questions that are often asked

Is stammering more common in boys than girls?

Yes, there are more boys who stammer, and the ratios quoted range between three to five boys to one girl (Kidd et al. 1978).

Can a child gradually or suddenly become fluent?

Yes, even when the symptoms are quite severe, many children can stop being disfluent as quickly as they started, or they may gradually acquire the skills of fluency as they become more competent in other areas of their development.

Why do some children speak well one day and then become very hesitant the next day?

Periods of disfluency are quite normal and can be associated, for example, with excitement, fatigue or uncertainty. Stammering is a fluctuating condition so that children can be fluent for days or weeks and then suddenly become disfluent again.

Does the stammering child differ from the fluent child?

It is not possible to state specific ways in which all children who stammer differ from those who are fluent, nor is it possible to say that all children who stammer do not differ psychologically or physically from those who are fluent. Stammering is not a single simple disorder, so that there are considerable variations in the children who stammer as well as in the speech symptoms that they display. The old idea that children who stammer are timid, shy, withdrawn and nervous has been found to be incorrect. There are indeed timid and nervous children who stammer, just as there are timid and nervous children who do not stammer. There are also confident and outgoing children who stammer, just as there are such children who are fluent.

Many questions remain unanswered regarding children who stammer, but research does indicate that these children may have more language and articulatory difficulties than fluent children; that more stammering children than fluent children may have anxious or demanding parents, and that there is a greater likelihood of stammering when there are relatives who stammer (Yairi and Ambrose 1999).

How can you help the young disfluent child?

Some dos and don'ts

There are a number of suggestions below and you may find one or two among these that can be implemented to help yourself or your child.

DON'T tell children to stop stammering or to talk more slowly – if they could they would. You will only cause confusion because they do not know how to stop.

DO remain as calm and patient as possible when the child stammers – if children are made fearful or tense, they may stammer more.

DO let children speak for themselves. If you speak for them or answer questions on their behalf, this will underline their inability to speak as efficiently and fluently as you do. They may feel more awkward when they have to speak for themselves.

DON'T say 'speak slowly', 'take a deep breath' or 'think before you speak'. This kind of advice may be helpful for that moment but, in the long term, it can create anxiety in the child and negative feelings about their ability to speak 'properly'.

DO behave in the same way with stammering children as with fluent ones. For example, a nursery teacher once said:

'It's all very well telling us these things, and they make sense, but in a room full of children with varying needs, it's difficult to know what to do for the best. For instance, I have a little boy called Billy in my group and two or three times a day he rushes up to me, wiggles about and looks agonised, and then says, "Please can I go to the t . . . t . . . t . . . t" and then he gets stuck.'

'What did you do?'

'I sent him off to the toilet, but I wasn't sure whether that was the right thing to do.'

This situation was discussed among a group of nursery nurses and teachers. It was decided that Billy was getting a reward for his behaviour and that he was being treated differently because of his speech. Had he been fluent, he would have been told to come and ask for the toilet in good time and not at the last moment. The advice given to the teacher by the group was to react quite normally the next time Billy approached her in this way and wait calmly for him to finish the word.

Some weeks later the nursery teacher reported that she had implemented the advice given and, on the first occasion, Billy looked amazed as he waited for her to send him to the toilet. Bravely, she stood her ground while he danced around. Finally, Billy started again and said, 'Please can I go to the t . . . t . . . t . . . toilet?' This teacher was well aware that Billy might have had an accident, but she was prepared to take the risk and is no longer treating Billy differently from the other children.

DON'T interrupt the child too much. We all have difficulty remembering what we are trying to say if we are constantly interrupted. A stammering child may become confused and give up speaking, or become much more disfluent.

DON'T call children 'stammerers' or label their speech as 'stammering'. We cannot give a guarantee that children will grow into the confirmed stage of stammering as they mature, so it is unnecessary to attach the stammering label. Once labelled, children may begin to accept the adults' evaluation and doubt their own abilities, and this may affect their performance. It may then not be clear whether the poor performance was due to a real difficulty, or due to anxiety caused by the label.

DO be a good speech model for children to copy as they will tend to speak as they are spoken to. Aim to keep your own speech calm and simple. Often our messages are too complicated for children to understand. For example:

'Hurry up now and tidy up your table, then make sure the guinea-pig has got water for the night, and get your coat because it is nearly going home time and we do not want to keep everyone waiting.'

Small children, especially disfluent ones, cannot cope with this barrage of instructions and information. Try to confine yourself to one or two simple instructions at a time.

DO reassure children who show real distress when they cannot say a word that, at times, everyone has difficulty with what they want to say. If adults accept a child's difficulties, so will the child. If the adults display concern and anxiety, so will the child.

DO react in the same way whether children are fluent or stammering. React to *what* they say and not to *how* they are saying it.

DO look for the things that the child can achieve and give plenty of praise.

Many highly successful people have stammered including Winston Churchill, Jonathan Miller, Lewis Carroll, Marilyn Monroe and Bruce Willis. The tall and the short, the fat and the thin, the beautiful and the not so beautiful, the fluent and the stammering – all can become successful providing they retain their self-confidence and self-esteem. No one is perfect, but when someone loses their self-confidence then every flaw becomes a major disaster. The more children are helped in these early years to build their confidence and self-esteem as whole human beings, and not on the basis of their fluent or disfluent speech, the more likely they are to get over the disfluent phase and, if this is impossible, to build a successful life without carrying the unnecessary burden of constant self-doubt and anxiety.

Further reading

The BSA (British Stammering Association) www.stammering.org

The Child who Stammers – information for parents
The Child who Stammers – information for teachers

Turnbull, J. and Stewart, T. (1996) *Helping Children Cope with Stammering*. London: Sheldon Press.

Chapter 6

Links Between Emotional/ Behavioural Problems and Communication Difficulties

Alison Wintgens

As children learn about the world and the people around them they must explore, experiment and test limits, which can be a trying time for even the most patient adult. This chapter looks beyond these expected behaviours, at children who are unusually difficult to manage and whose social and emotional development is giving cause for concern. It particularly considers:

- what is meant by the term 'emotional and behavioural problems';
- what sort of problems are likely;
- how common these are;
- why children with communication difficulties are especially prone;
- when and why some children have these problems;
- what can be done to help.

'Emotional and behavioural problems' – what does this mean?

Some stages in a child's early years are likely to be more demanding on the parents or carers than others – normal young toddlers can cling anxiously, older toddlers are often said to be 'into everything' and adults may resign themselves to the fact that 'it's the terrible twos'. Other adults may not have bargained for how lively many ordinary children are and insist that they are 'hyperactive' when they are showing normally energetic behaviour. In these examples the parents may need support and reassurance to help them through this stage if they are finding it difficult; but it is not helpful to call it an emotional or behavioural problem in the clinical sense since it is to be expected.

Clinically significant problems are more extensive or severe than behaviours or emotional reactions shown by the majority of children; and they interfere with children's ordinary lives and development, or cause them or other people considerable suffering. They are the sort of problems where it may be helpful to seek specialist help.

Therefore, when an adult feels that a child behaves in a way that causes concern, it is important to look at just how severe and extensive this behaviour is. Examples of the kinds of questions that might be asked are listed below under 'How can you help?' Broadly speaking, the degree of severity and its impact on the child or those around him or her will indicate whether this really is a clinically significant problem, and give an idea of how and who might help.

What types of problems may occur?

Most people notice a child who is difficult to manage, who challenges adults, or behaves in an antisocial way; their names can become infamous and even other young children may notice and go home with tales of what 'Rhys' or 'Bianca' did today! There are also those who are quieter and less obvious, but may be in just as much need of help – the child who seems withdrawn, depressed, immature or to be behaving in an odd or puzzling way.

There are various ways of classifying the problems commonly found in the birth to seven age group. The simplest is to identify two major divisions – behavioural problems and emotional problems – although children frequently show a mixture of the two.

Behavioural problems

The main behavioural problems are listed here.

> *Challenging parental control* – especially around discipline, such as at bedtimes, meal times, or on trips out.
>
> *Aggression* – excessive tantrums, which may be verbal or physical, including behaviour such as hitting, scratching, biting, or deliberately destructive behaviour.
>
> *Activity* – an increased level of activity commonly coupled with a lack of concentration.
>
> *Feeding* – such as refusing food which may lead to failure to thrive (failing to grow and gain weight) or pica (eating inappropriate objects) – for example, the child who eats very little and whose weight is very low, or one who eats, for example, worms and other insects.

Sleeping – taking a long time to get off to sleep, or waking at night.
Toilet training – wetting (also known as enuresis) or soiling (encopresis) beyond the age at which a child should be dry and clean.

Emotional problems

There are basically two areas.

Anxiety – such as problems of separation from the mother, or persistent irrational fears like imagining there is a monster under the bed.
Depression – a miserable appearance, or excessive crying.

How common are they?

Such difficulties are common. Various surveys (Richman *et al.* 1982; Rutter *et al.* 1975) suggest that 5 to 10 per cent of children have a clinically significant emotional and/or behavioural problem at some stage in their childhood, children from cities being the most vulnerable. An overview of more recent studies points on average to a slightly higher figure of 12.3 per cent (Verhulst 1995).

Why children with communication problems are particularly prone to emotional and behavioural problems

The link between emotional and behavioural problems and speech and language problems is strong and complex. It is easy to see a number of connections:

(a) children with comprehension problems may not do what they are told because they do not understand, and thus get into trouble;
(b) children who cannot make themselves understood because of unclear speech or limited expressive language may withdraw, or get so frustrated they have frequent temper tantrums;
(c) children who are withdrawn do not spend as much time practising talking to others as sociable children do, and so may have delayed language development;
(d) children who are abused or neglected may have more difficulties with language and communication skills.

In these examples it seems possible to see cause and effect. In examples (a) and (b) there is a primary communication problem. In examples (c) and (d) there is a secondary communication problem.

However, the position may become increasingly complex, like a vicious circle, with both aspects closely interwoven, and it is often not possible nor helpful to say what is primary and what is secondary.

Some experts (Prizant *et al.* 1990) have suggested four other ways in which emotional and behavioural problems, and speech and language are related.

1. They can co-occur, with or without obvious ties, as in the child with delayed language and depression where the two may be linked. Another child with delayed language may have sleeping problems, but these two may be unconnected.
2. The communication problem can be an essential part of the diagnosis, as in autism.
3. The communication problem can be an associated part of the diagnosis, as in learning disability.
4. The communication problem can be the sole part of the diagnosis, as in stammering (see Chapter 5).

Why does it happen?

It is known (Graham *et al.* 1999) that the commonest causes of emotional and behavioural problems in early childhood are disharmonious family relationships, inconsistent or harsh child-rearing practices, and critical or hostile parental attitudes. However, it is important to stress that there are many children whose families do not fall into these categories.

In addition, most experts would agree that it is unusual to find a single clear-cut cause for a child's emotional and/or behavioural problem. As well as interactions between the child and family there are the child's interactions with the wider environment, and factors present within the child.

It may be helpful to plot possible causes on a grid such as Table 6.1 below. Predisposing factors are any things in the past or within the child's make-up that affect the child's behaviour or emotional state. Precipitating causes occur immediately before the emotional or behaviour problem is noticed. Perpetuating factors are those that seem to maintain the behaviour that is causing concern.

Table 6.1 Causes of emotional/behavioural problems

Factors	Child	Family	Wider environment
Predisposing	D	C	
Precipitating			A, B
Perpetuating			E, B

Imagine a little boy who appears to be miserable and withdrawn following the death of his much loved guinea-pig three months previously. This is shown as A in Table 6.1. The death of the guinea-pig is a precipitating factor. However, several other relevant causes come to light during a thorough initial interview with the family:

B – the child has been bullied at school for several months (precipitating and perpetuating factors);
C – his maternal grandmother died nine months ago, and his mother finds it hard to talk about death (predisposing factor);
D – he has always had a rather introverted temperament (predisposing factor);
E – the child experienced another loss when his main friend at school recently moved away from the area (perpetuating factor).

Understanding all the various causes is essential in order to know how to help. Knowing about the grandmother's death; knowing the child's temperament; counselling for the mother; strategies to manage the bullying, and help with social skills to build up friendships may all play a part.

Let us look at the three headings in Table 6.1 in more detail.

The child

The child may have been born with a serious primary condition such as autism, or learning disability where the emotional and/or behavioural problems may be part of the condition.

There may be a physical problem such as cerebral palsy, deafness, or epilepsy, or an injury such as severe burns, all of which may restrict the child physically or socially, or arouse unhelpful attitudes from family or friends.

Temperamental factors may be significant. The child may not be placid and adaptable but have characteristics more vulnerable to stress or change.

The family

One could imagine that a child with an emotional and/or behavioural problem may come from a family whose lifestyle appears chaotic, rigid, or harsh, or from a family which is considered to be deprived. Certainly the family environment, the quality of close relationships, and parental attitudes are very important to developing children. They have to move from complete dependence to independence, and for this to happen there needs to be a gradual transfer of responsibility from the adults to the children. Children's backgrounds should therefore be secure, stable, stimulating and reasonably consistent. They will be at risk of emotional and/or behavioural problems if the family relationships or members are very disturbed, or there are a lot of changes or stresses.

Going back a generation, a lot can depend on what experiences the parents themselves had as children. Unfortunately, all too often, it may be that their own family relationships were disturbed, and that possibly the pattern is being repeated. Sometimes parents make a big effort to avoid what they see as their parents' mistakes, but with no model to go by they may swing to the opposite extreme, or be inconsistent.

The wider environment

This area covers all other people, places or activities with which the child is involved. Events or relationships at school, nursery, or playgroup may be the cause of difficulty or distress for the child. Frequent changes of teacher, going to stay with a friend, or bullying are all examples in this category.

Child abuse

It seems necessary to mention child abuse separately here, with the steady increase in the number of reported cases of child abuse and neglect in recent years. Whether predisposing, precipitating or perpetuating, within or outside the family, the effects of maltreatment are likely to cause or contribute to a child's emotional and/or behavioural problem.

Although many children suffer several forms of abuse, it may be helpful to clarify the four main types:

1. physical, or non-accidental injury, where children are physically injured or damaged not as the result of an accident;
2. emotional, where parents so threaten or verbally abuse children that they become very fearful;

3. neglect, where parents fail to protect children or to provide an adequate environment for their development;
4. sexual, when sexually mature people involve children in any sexual activity.

How can you help children with emotional/behavioural problems?

Documenting the problem and understanding how and why it occurs

1. Watch the child carefully and see, as exactly as possible, what the problem is, how, when and with whom it happens and how often.

   It is easy, for example, to turn round and see Ben hitting Fasila. But this could have happened in a number of ways, such as: a seemingly unprovoked attack; tit-for-tat paying back which Fasila started; or Ben's attempt to defend his younger sister whom Fasila just accidentally knocked over.

   Close observations make it much easier to describe a problem, deal with it, and to tell if it is getting better or worse. It may be helpful to describe the behaviour bearing in mind a simplified version of the 'ABC'. This ABC method is a part of 'Behaviour Modification' (Herbert 1996), a way of treating children's behaviour problems frequently used by psychologists. A are the Antecedents, or what came immediately before the incident, what exactly the child and relevant others were doing. B is the Behaviour itself – what exactly the child does, the place, time, situation and people involved. C are the Consequences, what exactly other people do or say as a result of the behaviour. Changing the antecedents or the consequences will result in changes to the behaviour.

2. Get a description of the 'problem' from all angles by talking to others involved with the child – parents, other close family members, teachers, nursery nurses, therapists or other carers. Ask the following questions:

   - What exactly happens?
   - With whom does the 'problem' exist?
   - To what extent does it affect different aspects of the child's and family's lives?
   - Is the child's development affected?

3. Find out how concerned other people are. You might ask:

- Who is most worried?
- How worried are they?

This will give you an idea of the severity of the problem, whether you should turn to specialists for help, and how motivated the parents are to change things.

4. Ask what people have done to try and solve the problem. Ask, 'What do you do when Hassan won't eat?' or ' . . . when Lucy screams?' Get an idea of various solutions people have attempted and how well they have worked. In this way you may not only get an idea of a new and helpful solution, but also a chance to see how consistently the problem is handled.

Using simple management tactics

Handling difficult behaviour

Difficult behaviour often happens quickly and needs to be dealt with immediately. There may be little time to think out the best solution and your reaction to it might be almost a reflex. Nevertheless, here are a few principles and suggestions for managing difficult behaviour, along with a warning that the behaviour may seem to get worse at first if you change your way of dealing with it, but in the long term there will be definite improvements and benefits.

- Ignore when (and if!) possible.
- Try to keep as calm as possible – if a child is deliberately trying to annoy you, don't show them they have pressed the right button!
- Divert and distract especially if the child is younger, or if you catch a situation early enough and anticipate trouble ahead.
- Set clear limits and stick to them – for example, if you ask a child to put away some toys see it through, even if you have to give a lot of encouragement, or a little help.
- Choose only the most important things to correct – if you constantly tell a child off it loses its effect.
- Explain briefly why you are telling a child to do (or not to do) something – 'because I say so' teaches them nothing.
- Make explanations and instructions short and simple, especially if the child is quite young, or may have a language problem.
- Be specific – tell him/her exactly what you want rather than a vague instruction to 'be a good boy/girl.'

- Tell (instruct), don't ask, if you want something done – 'Are you going to pick that up?' invites the answer, 'No!'
- Give clear messages – for example if you say, 'No, don't do that,' make sure your face is serious with no hint of laughing.
- Show that you are pleased with praise, smiles, hugs or whatever when the child is behaving well or has done what was asked such as played quietly, shared a toy or said sorry to someone.
- Use your voice, face and body to reinforce the message you want to get across.
- Find out and talk about the feelings that are underlying the behaviour, so the child learns that the feelings are acceptable but the behaviour is not. For example, you might say, 'I know you're feeling cross because we can't go to the park, but you're not to (deliberately) spill your drink.'
- Only use sanctions, like 'time out', for extreme behaviours that cannot be ignored, such as kicking or hitting.
- Think the best of children and try and see it their way – if they do not do what they are told try and think why, rather than assume they are disobedient; there may be a conflict of interests or a lack of understanding, rather than a deliberate attempt to provoke.

Some other handling suggestions
The following suggestions may come in useful with children who are shy or withdrawn, very active, or lacking in motivation.
- Try and get very active children to stick at a task for just half a minute more, or to look at just one more page of a book. Build it up gradually rather than be unrealistic and expect them to concentrate for a quarter of an hour, or finish a whole book.
- If children won't pay attention or play with what you want them to, get involved in what they are doing and try and adapt that for your purposes. Start where the child is and gradually help them tolerate adult involvement, or gradually move on to your choice of task.
- Don't pay extra attention to shy children – it only makes it worse. Leave them to join in or speak in their own time, and give plenty of reassurance.
- Interesting or adult-like equipment can help with a child who has poor attention or concentration – for example, a calculator instead of dice to encourage a seven-year-old to try a board game; or a bulldog type clip for a preschool child to use to hold pictures or cards.
- With children with poor talking and/or low self-esteem, respond

and give encouragement for the smallest thing they contribute, and watch for their non-verbal attempts as well.

• Prepare children for change, whether it is a change of routine, a new significant adult in their lives, or a different arrangement of a familiar room. Many children – and adults – find change difficult, especially if they are emotionally vulnerable, so give warning and involve children in preparations for change.

Helping parents

1. *Don't just give bad news.* If you need to talk to parents about something that bothers you – perhaps the child never joins in group activities, seems to be a loner and has poor concentration – it is usually helpful to talk about how the child is getting on in general. That way there is a chance for the parents to hear some good news about the child as well as what you are worried about.

2. *Work in partnership with the parents* sharing information and discussing solutions or changes. They know the child best and are the ones who have to live with him/her and have to find a way of managing him/her which works and with which they are happy (see Chapter 10).

3. *Find a common language.* If parents say, 'It's her moods that worry us,' make sure that you, they, and the child, if she is old enough, all know exactly what is meant by the word 'moods', for example, 'When she puts on a sulky face, sits doing nothing and won't talk to anyone.'

4. *Avoid blaming either parent or child.* The chances are that it is the way in which one particular child interacts with one or both particular parent(s), and a combination of several causes as was discussed earlier. With that in mind you can avoid blame and guilt, which are not helpful in solving the problem.

5. *Support parents and boost their confidence.* Remember that it can be miserable for parents if their child does not behave in an acceptable way and may lead to a feeling of guilt and failure. Praise what is going well, and encourage the parents.

6. *Try and find a solution that the parents are trying, or want to try.* Parents often do have the answers, but sometimes they lack confidence or staying power. Maybe they have been undermined by someone from the generation above who has stepped in to try and help; or maybe they feel that what they try never seems to work, although it may well do if they stick to one thing and see it through consistently.

Referral for further help

If you and/or the family have tried to manage the problem yourselves and are still worried you should look for outside help.

Several specialists are available to advise on children's emotional and behavioural problems. Who you turn to may depend on the setting the child is in, for example, nursery, clinic or school, or where the family lives.

The most obvious specialists are:

– specialist health visitors or doctors running sleep and behaviour clinics – for preschool children;

– educational psychologist – if the problem is within school;

– clinical psychologist;

– child mental health professionals in a multidisciplinary team – if the problem is severe and persistent.

Referrals are usually made via the school, health visitor, community doctor, therapist or GP. Before referring, many specialists welcome a telephone call to discuss whether they are the most suitable person/team to turn to. A referral letter with a good description of the problem is necessary, and sometimes the referrer is invited to the first appointment so that all concerns can be discussed openly with the family. For any treatment to be effective, it is important that parents recognise the difficulties, and want to change them themselves, not just to keep the nursery, the social worker or whoever quiet.

Conclusion

Emotional and behavioural problems should always be taken seriously. Many of them are surprisingly persistent and it cannot be assumed that reassurance, and the attitude that a child will always 'grow out of it', will be enough. Even common problems, like waking at night, can be very draining on a family.

Nevertheless, facing up to these problems and working with the children and their families is very worthwhile. Understanding children's emotional and social development and their behaviour, as well as interactions within families, are fascinating areas of study. The improvements that can be seen as a result of successful management have enormous benefits for the child and family.

Further reading

Herbert, M. (1996) *The PACTS (Parent, Adolescent and Child Training Skills) series*. Leicester: BPS Books (The British Psychological Society).
A series of 12 booklets including titles on feeding problems and bedtime battles, toilet training, social skills training, setting limits, feuding and fighting, supporting bereaved and dying children, separation and divorce.

Webster-Stratton, C. (1992) *The Incredible Years – A Trouble-shooting Guide for Parents of Children Aged 3–8*. Toronto, Canada: Umbrella Press.

Chapter 7

The Speech and Language Therapist

Jannet A. Wright

Speech and language therapists are the professionals who are contacted if a child is known to have a speech and language problem or if parents and/or teachers are concerned about the way in which a child communicates (RCSLT 1996).

In the UK the majority of speech and language therapists are employed by the National Health Service. Therapists may work in nurseries, health centres and hospitals although many now work in schools, including mainstream schools and special schools such as schools for deaf children, physically disabled children, or children with learning disabilities.

Some therapists specialise in working with children from multicultural backgrounds where English is an additional language. Such children may have difficulties learning the language spoken at home as well as English. A therapist will not see them unless they are having problems in both their first language and English. The therapist will need to ascertain the level of the child's difficulties in the first language by gathering information from the parents and the child, often using interpreters or co-workers. If children have a problem in their first language as well as in learning English, then the speech and language therapist will work with the families to help the children develop the underlying skills necessary for language learning.

As stated in Chapter 2, communication begins at birth, so therapists may be asked to see children from birth onwards. Therapists may become involved with children and their families very early in the children's development. This may be to help with communication or if there are any feeding problems such as those associated with a cleft lip and/or palate or a physical problem that has been identified at birth. See suggested further reading at the end of this chapter for specific information regarding feeding and cleft lip and/or palate.

A speech and language therapist investigates children's speech and language in order to establish their communicative abilities as well as to define the difficulties they may be having with communication. Each child will be looked at individually. The therapist will also consider the patterns of interaction in the family. This enables the therapist not only to identify the problems that the child is having with communication, but also to look at any features in the child's environment that may be contributing to these difficulties. The therapist will discuss with the parents their child's communication and work out with them the best way to help their child.

If the child attends a school or a nursery the therapist will, with the parents' permission, talk to the teachers about how the child communicates with the staff as well as with other children. In this situation the therapist will want to work with the teachers and the parents to help the child. It is also important for the therapist to ensure that ideas for therapy which may arise from the speech and language assessment can be integrated with the curriculum topics and teaching methods used in the school.

Increasingly therapists are being asked to train others to work with children who have communication problems. This may include parents as well as practitioners in the early years.

Referral to speech and language therapy

Speech and language therapists will usually have a base for administrative purposes and where messages may be left for them, although they may work in several different places during each week.

Children may be referred to a speech and language therapist by their parents. Other sources of referral include the GP, health visitors, teachers or any other concerned professional. The professional who refers a child to speech and language therapy will hopefully have explained to the parents the reason for such a referral. A speech and language therapist cannot see a child unless the parents have given their permission.

Service delivery

The local arrangements for speech and language therapy service provision are influenced by the demands of the National Health Service, the local education authority and the schools. This means that the organisation of services will vary from one geographical area to another. Thus, for example, a child with a communication problem who lives in Yorkshire may come into contact with a service organised in a different way from a child with the same problem who lives in Cornwall.

There is also variation in the way in which therapists work. In some areas therapists will work directly with the children while in other areas therapists work 'indirectly', training others to continue therapy with the children.

Health Centre based services

Even within one geographical area speech and language therapists may vary the frequency of the appointments that they offer. This will depend on the needs of the child, the family's commitments, the therapist's rationale for the management of that child and the policy and organisation of the local services. The length of time that children and their families spend with a therapist will vary, depending on the needs of the children. Sometimes an appointment will last 30 to 45 minutes, whereas some appointments may last up to one and a half hours.

Children may be seen as part of a group when they may be asked to attend for a whole morning or an afternoon. Parents are expected to bring their children for the appointment so that they may be able to join in the therapy. This then means that the work the speech and language therapist does with the child can be continued at home on a daily basis. During the session there may be time to encourage parents to practise certain activities in order that these may then be continued at home. Parents need to be involved as much as possible from the time of referral.

Intensive courses may be offered during the school holidays. Children attend such courses on a daily basis in the summer or at Easter and parents may also be asked to attend.

School based services

In an increasing number of areas speech and language therapists are working within mainstream schools where they liaise directly with the teachers and learning support assistants. The teacher and therapist will discuss the effect of the communication problem on the child's academic work (Wright and Kersner 1998). They will also decide how therapy may be incorporated into curricular activities and how relevant new vocabulary and topics may be used as a part of therapy. Sometimes therapists may work with an individual child or a group of children within the classroom. Often, the therapist will train a classroom assistant or learning support assistant to continue regular therapy.

In some areas children attending mainstream schools may go to the local health centre for speech and language therapy appointments, although this means that they have to take time off school. If a child attends a special school or a language unit within a mainstream school, a speech and language therapist may be based there and therapy will always be offered within the school environment.

Some of the children seen by a speech and language therapist may have a Statement of Special Educational Need to which the therapist may have contributed a report. The provision of speech and language therapy may be either the main need of the child, or one of many.

What will the speech and language therapist do?

The therapist will need to assess the child and to ask the parent questions relating to the child's environment and background.

The therapist will need to ask the parents about their child's development and health in order to see if there are any links between the communication problems and general development. The therapist will also be interested in who referred the child and why, so that the problem can be seen through the eyes of the person who made the referral.

The speech and language therapist will want to know the results of the child's latest hearing test. In some cases this may involve arranging further assessments before therapy can begin. This is to establish whether the child's problems are related to any hearing difficulties.

Assessment

The speech and language therapist needs to obtain a complete picture of the child, including speech and language skills. The assessment of communication problems involves using materials with which children are comfortable, namely toys and books. The way in which they play can reveal a great deal about the way in which they think and understand the world around them, and aspects of their intellectual functioning. The therapist will also be interested in the children's attention, how long they play with one toy, their interaction skills and their non-verbal communication such as gestures, pointing and eye contact.

The child's language development will be discussed with the parents. Therapists need to know how children speak, what they understand and what they talk about. The way in which children relate to other people will also be of interest.

Understanding

The therapist will try to work out how much a child understands, using a variety of assessment techniques. It may appear that children 'understand everything that is said to them' (see Chapter 4) but if situational clues are removed they may have more difficulty. Formal tests may be used to reduce the clues children can utilise, and scores on a particular test may be converted into 'age equivalent' scores so that the performance of children of a similar age can be compared.

Expression

During the speech and language therapy session the therapist may, with the parents' agreement, use a tape recorder to collect examples of children's language. These language samples will be analysed by the therapist after the session. They can then be considered in detail and compared to developmental norms in order to identify children's communication strengths and weaknesses. The therapist will note the grammatical structures as well as the vocabulary that children use.

Speech sounds

While therapists analyse these language samples they also listen to the speech sounds the children use. If this is an area of particular concern therapists will ask children to name some pre-selected pictures that will provide examples of pronunciation of a wide range of sounds. The therapist will study the production of single words and words in continuous speech, as in the language sample, to see if there is a pattern in the way certain sounds are produced, omitted or substituted. Again the therapist will compare each child's speech to known developmental patterns in order to plan therapy.

Interaction

Therapists frequently use videos to record the ways in which children interact with their parents and siblings as this helps the therapists to assess and understand the full range of the children's communicative abilities. Videos may also be used during therapy sessions to help parents identify their own strengths in the ways in which they interact with their child and to highlight areas which need to be changed (see also Chapters 9 and 10).

Team assessment

Sometimes the speech and language therapist works with other professionals such as paediatricians, psychologists and teachers in order to gain a complete picture of the child. A group of professionals may form a team that comes together as required by the needs of an individual child; or the team may be one that works together consistently and is for example based in a hospital or child development centre. In the latter case this may help to reduce the number of hospital appointments a family has to attend and parents may see the therapist at the same time as other professionals.

Integrating speech and language therapy

Speech and language therapy sessions will only be successful if the therapy is then integrated into a child's life style. If speech and language therapy is offered in a school setting the therapist faces the same issues that arise for other support services. For example they will have to make decisions about seeing the children in the classroom or taking them out into another room for therapy. They will have to arrange a time to talk to the teacher and/or assistant. Such negotiations are potentially time consuming but are necessary if a child is to receive a coordinated programme of intervention from therapists and education staff. Only with such coordination will children with speech and language problems receive the consistent support which will enable them to integrate their newly acquired skills into their everyday lives.

Further reading

Harding, A. and Sell, D. (2001) 'Cleft palate and velopharyngeal anomalies', in Kersner, M. and Wright, J. A. (eds) *Speech and Language Therapy: The decision-making process when working with children*, 215–30. London: David Fulton Publishers.

Law, J. (2002) *Trouble Talking,* 2nd edn. London: Jessica Kingsley Publishers.

Winstock, A. (1994) *The Practical Management of Eating and Drinking Difficulties in Children.* Bicester: Winslow Press/Speechmark.

Chapter 8

Language Programmes

Rachel Rees

A language programme may refer to any structured framework that encourages communication development in young children. There are now many published language programmes that may take the form of books or kits. It is helpful if such published programmes are seen as a potential resource, rather than a curriculum to be followed from start to finish with all children that have communication difficulties. Selecting programmes that may prove to be a good resource for the children with whom you are working is not necessarily an easy task.

Questions that may guide the selection of a published language programme

- Can the programme be used by a range of professionals and parents working together?
- Can activities in the programme be integrated into daily life and a teaching curriculum?
- Is the programme based on sound theories concerning language development?
- Does the programme utilise strategies that are used to encourage normal language development?
- Does the programme provide practical ideas that have been tried and tested?
- Do the activities motivate children by engaging their interest?
- Does the programme include activities that fulfil the needs of the child or children you are considering?
- Is the programme flexible and clearly categorised so that it can be used as a resource?

Selection should therefore be guided by knowledge of normal language development and the strategies that encourage it, as well as by a careful assessment of a child or group of children. Selected programmes and activities within them often need to be adapted and combined with other approaches. Ideas and activities taken from published language programmes should be integrated with the child's daily activities and teaching curriculum. This selection and integration process is best done by professionals working together, such as speech and language therapists working with nursery staff and parents.

This chapter provides information about a selection of published language programmes that fulfil most of the criteria discussed above. The programmes were selected following a survey in which practising speech and language therapists were asked which programmes they commonly used as a resource. The selection provides a range of resources although it is not a definitive list.

For each of the programmes, the aims and format are described and the practical nature of the programme is illustrated by providing examples of approaches and activities. This should enable the reader to select programmes they wish to investigate further and to gain some general practical ideas.

Individual books

Early Communication Skills (second edition) by Charlotte Lynch and Julia Kidd

This activity book is one of the popular *Early Skills* series published by Speechmark. It aims to provide professionals and parents with practical ideas for encouraging pre-verbal and early verbal communication skills. The activities are based on approaches used by the authors, a teacher of the deaf and a speech and language therapist, when they were working together with deaf children in a nursery. Some of the sections are more applicable to deaf children but many are useful for all groups of children. The book is clearly divided into nine sections and in each the activities are in approximate developmental order.

The nine sections are:

- Pre-verbal Skills
- Language and Play
- Early Listening: Awareness of Sound
- Early Listening: Awareness of Voice
- Vocalisations
- Auditory Discrimination

- Speech Discrimination
- Auditory/Visual Memory
- Early Words

Each section or subsection is introduced with an explanation of the importance in communication development of the skill described and there are some general tips on how that skill can be encouraged in everyday activities. This is followed by a list of practical activities and games. Each section ends with photocopiable record sheets.

Here are some examples:

1. The first pre-verbal skill described is eye contact. The authors explain how looking at the speaker's face helps the child to gain information about language through facial expression and, in the case of deaf children, through lip patterns, gestures and signs. They explain that communication can break down if the child is not looking at the adult and so the adult assumes the child is not interested in what they are communicating. General tips on improving eye contact in young children include suggesting that the adults try to make their facial expressions more interesting for the children and try to wait before giving them a drink to encourage the children to look up at them. Activities to encourage eye contact include games that involve hiding and revealing the face and songs that can be interrupted to wait for eye contact before continuing.

2. In the section on 'early words' the authors explain how children need to hear a word many times and in many different situations before they learn it. One of the general tips they give concerning early word learning is not to spoil the child's enjoyment of a game by insisting on an attempt at a word. A list of words learnt early in development is divided into eight categories and, for many of these words, the authors suggest various games and activities where the child can repeatedly hear the word in context. For example, the following activities are suggested to encourage the child to acquire the action word 'gone': emphasising the word when toys disappear by covering objects with a scarf; hiding finger puppets behind your back, and rolling a ball across a table into a tin.

These examples illustrate how the suggestions and activities can be used by professionals and parents with a range of young children in everyday situations at home or in a nursery or playgroup.

Early Listening Skills by Diana Williams

This activity book is another of Speechmark's *Early Skills* series. It is designed mainly for preschool children with delayed listening skills and many of the activities are particularly useful for children with a hearing loss. The author stresses that activities and strategies chosen should be compatible with the child's auditory and language abilities. Therefore the book is intended for professionals working with this group of children.

The first ten chapters cover auditory detection, discrimination, recognition, sequencing and memory. There are also sections covering suggested listening topics for the school curriculum and holiday listening projects. Sections consist mainly of suggested strategies and activities, and record sheets, all of which are photocopiable.

Here are some examples:

1. There are suggestions for drawing a child's attention to sounds in and around the home and a checklist of sounds is provided for parents such as 'key in the door' and 'cutlery put away in the drawer'.
2. There are many suggestions for activities that involve children waiting for a verbal or non-verbal signal before they respond, such as waiting for a croak before they make a cut-out frog jump into a bucket.
3. There are activities to encourage children to discriminate between different musical sounds and rhythms. Activities for discriminating speech mainly involve attention and listening to known words. For example, in a suggested activity where the child is helping to pack a suitcase for a teddy, the child is asked to name the clothing items first. Any items the child is unable to name are discarded. The child is then asked to fetch the named items and put them in the case.

Developing Baseline Communication Skills by Catherine Delamain and Jill Spring

This activity book has been designed to relate to the baseline assessments in primary schools. It consists mainly of practical activities to use in school settings. The nature of the activities reflects the wide work experience of the authors, both speech and language therapists who have worked closely with teachers. The activities are divided into two sections:

Personal and Social Development Activities

* turn taking;
* body language;

- awareness of others;
- confidence and independence;
- feelings and emotions.

Language and Literacy Activities

- understanding;
- listening and attention;
- speaking;
- auditory memory;
- phonological awareness (awareness of how words are made up of syllables and sounds).

Each section is divided into four levels. At each level five activities are clearly described on separate pages. Each page indicates the section, the level and the area of the timetable/curriculum in which the activity can be used. These areas cover circle time, hall/PE, literacy, topic work, drama and small group work.

Many of the activities encourage child-to-child talk and many need little, if any, equipment. Record sheets are provided and most of the pages in the book are photocopiable.

Here is an example of an activity for *Listening and Attention, Level 1* that can be used in circle time and for small group work:

Children are given simple commands such as 'touch your nose'. They are told to wait until they hear the word 'go', which follows the command after a pause. The volume of 'go' and the length of the pause can vary to increase or decrease the level of difficulty.

Working with Children's Language (revised edition) by Jackie Cooke and Diana Williams

This book belongs to Speechmark's *Working With* series and is designed for young children who have delayed language, but who are developing normally in other areas. It can be used by speech and language therapists and others involved with such children.

There are six chapters covering the following aspects of language and language-related skills:

- Early Language Skills (e.g. babbling, first words, symbolic understanding, attention sharing and the concept of cause and effect);
- Attention Control and Listening Skills (e.g. attracting and sustaining attention and shifting attention);

- Play Skills (e.g. physical play skills, imaginative play skills);
- Comprehension Skills (e.g. relating two verbal concepts, understanding pronouns);
- Expressive Language Skills (e.g. using two word phrases, using negatives);
- Perception Skills (e.g. visual sequencing, general auditory awareness, auditory memory).

Each chapter is divided into three parts:

- theory;
- guidelines to remediation;
- activities.

The activities are mainly a collection of those frequently used by educators of young children. The way they are categorised and linked to the theory enables the user to find a range of practical ideas. It also helps users to target specific skills that may have been identified by an assessment of the child's language.

Here is an example of how theory is linked to practical ideas:

In the sections on 'cause and effect' the theory includes a description of the normal development of this concept. Parents usually help their children to recognise the connection between their own actions and the result of that action by helping them to manipulate toys and drawing the children's attention to the result.

There is also a discussion of objects that do something exciting as a result of a small manipulation. These items include music boxes, volume controls on the radio and pull-along toys that make a noise. Guidelines are given which suggest that parents give plenty of demonstrations. When the children seem interested, it is suggested that the parents might help them to manipulate the object by guiding their hand or moving the object towards them.

Working with Pragmatics by Lucie Andersen-Wood and Benita Rae Smith

This book closely integrates theoretical information on pragmatics (use of language) with practical ideas. Although this can make it more difficult to find practical tips quickly, it does enable users to be clear about why they are using certain types of intervention.

For example, there are suggestions for ways in which adults may alter their interaction style and ideas for how they may adapt everyday activities to encourage communication. In a section on drawing/illustration there are various suggestions for encouraging communication at home, in a class/group and in real life situations. It is suggested that:

- adults could take a non-directive interest in the child's drawings at home, making comments about which drawings they particularly like or about the colour or shape, rather than always asking, 'What's that?'
- 'polaroid' photographs of class outings could be used to encourage children to talk to each other;
- adults could encourage awareness of public displays as a talking point;
- adults could encourage children to make patterns on beaches or sandy areas for others to find later and talk about this.

For slightly older children there are ideas for increasing the child's awareness of the nature and effects of pragmatic skills and suggestions about how to teach these skills more directly. The book includes forms to photocopy for assessment and profiling.

Kits

Kits are described as programmes that consist of more than one book and may include separate assessment pictures, assessment/record forms, resource/activity books and videocassettes.

It Takes Two to Talk by Ayala Manolson

This is one of the programmes produced by the Hanen Centre, a charitable organisation based in Canada that is committed to helping young children communicate more effectively (www.hanen.org). In order to run an official Hanen programme, the trainer must attend a relevant course and be certified by the Hanen Centre. However, many professionals incorporate ideas and resources from parts of the Hanen programmes into their own work.

It Takes Two to Talk was the first parent–child interaction programme to be produced by the Hanen Centre and it is now the most widely used, implemented by many Hanen certified speech and language therapists in the UK.

The introduction to the parents' guide explains that many of the most natural reactions to communication breakdown are not necessarily helpful to the child, for example taking over control of the conversation. The parent guidebook provides practical advice on effective ways in which parents may take indirect action. It encourages them to:

- observe children;
- wait for and notice their attempts at communication;
- listen;
- follow their lead;
- take turns;
- respond and keep the conversation going;
- create opportunities for communication through games, play, music, art, sharing books and other activities.

Reference is made to how communication develops so that parents understand the importance of these skills.

The official programme lasts 12 to 13 weeks and includes eight weekly group training sessions and three individual feedback sessions. Group sessions involve experiential learning including interactive lectures, analysis of video recordings that are included in the pack, and discussions. Parents are encouraged to try out specific strategies between sessions and to share ideas and learn from each other. The parent guidebook includes clear descriptions of the strategies and their importance and gives explicit advice on how to implement them using scenarios, illustrations and simple 'do' and 'don't' instructions.

Here is one of the scenarios used to illustrate the importance of observation:

A mother lifted up her child so that she could see her reflection in the mirror, commenting on what she was doing. However, the child kept looking below the mirror. The mother followed the child's gaze and noticed that she was looking at a bowl of flowers underneath the mirror. The mother and child then spent time smelling the flowers together.

The last sections of the parent guidebook relating to communication opportunities contain songs and rhymes, ideas for activities and more explicit advice on useful strategies. For example, when sharing books, the following suggestions are given:

- choose a book that matches the child's level of understanding;
- choose a book that has pictures that enhance the story;
- find some real objects that are pictured in the book so that the child can see them and touch them;
- let the child turn the pages and choose the pictures he/she wants to look at.

The last part of the guidebook includes record sheets that parents can use. These cannot be photocopied but could be used as models from which to draw ideas.

You Make the Difference by Ayala Manolson, Barb Ward and Nancy Dodington

This programme is also produced by the Hanen Centre and is based on *It Takes Two to Talk* (Manolson 1992). Therefore it has similar aims and format and again trainers must attend a relevant course. It also consists of a parent guidebook and accompanying teaching videotape. This programme was designed specifically for preschool children at risk of developing language problems and is a community-based programme. For this reason it is sometimes used in the UK as a resource on government-funded Sure Start programmes (www.surestart.gov.uk).

The official *You Make the Difference* programme includes nine weekly sessions that the children and their parents attend. This includes group learning for the parents while their children are cared for by qualified staff, as well as time for the parents to practise what they are learning and be given feedback. The programme aims to empower parents by helping them to recognise that they have the ability to foster their child's communication skills. The guidebook uses simple language and colourful and humorous cartoons, making it more accessible for parents who have first languages other than English.

Learning Language and Loving It by Elaine Weitzman

This Hanen programme is designed for educators, rather than parents, and aims to promote the social, language and early literacy development of all young children.

As with the other adaptations of *It Takes Two to Talk* it follows the philosophies and principles of the first Hanen programme. It consists of a guidebook and videotape. The official programme, run by certified trainers, includes seven group training sessions and six individual videotaping and feedback sessions. The training sessions cover the programme content through interactive teaching, and the videotaping and feedback sessions help the educators to apply specific strategies and develop self-evaluation skills.

The skills covered include:

- interacting with children with different communication styles;
- observing children, waiting for and listening to any attempts made to communicate;

- helping children to become conversational partners in one-to-one and group situations;
- adjusting communication to help children understand;
- encouraging enjoyment of books.

The guidebook explains the importance and effect of using these skills and provides practical advice and exercises to help the reader understand how to put theory into practice.

Here are some examples.

One of the strategies for encouraging peer interaction is 'setting up interactions from outside the group'. The following scenario is described to illustrate this (pages 170–71):

A boy is annoying three girls in the home corner by repeatedly smashing his wagon against the side of the house. The teacher suggests he fills his wagon with toy tools and goes back to the house with him, knocks on the door and informs the girls that a man has come to fix their stove. She then encourages the boy to fix the stove and the girls then tell him that the fridge isn't working either!

This kind of strategy would be very useful to use with a child with communication difficulties who was becoming socially isolated.

The advantages of extending the topic for children with more advanced language are outlined. It is suggested that a topic can be extended by informing, projecting, explaining, talking about the future, talking about feelings or pretending and imagining.

Some sections of the guidebook are specifically related to children learning English as an additional language, children with language delay and children with special needs. Strategies that are explained and illustrated include:

- providing intensive repetition;
- timing responses to correspond to focus of attention,
- using contrasts to highlight the rule.

Social Use of Language Programme for Primary and Infant School Children by Wendy Rinaldi

This programme is designed to be implemented by teaching or therapy professionals. It is recommended to attend a training course but this is not a requirement for using the programme. A revised and extended version will be available from 2003.

The programme aims to help children learn social skills such as eye contact, listening and turn taking, which are essential for effective inter-action. It includes procedures for assessment and recording progress, story-books, suggested activities and lesson plan guides.

It is important for children to understand the effects of different social skills. The concepts of good social skills and poor social skills are intro-duced and explained through story-books. Here the range of skills covered is put into the context of early uses of language such as taking messages and expressing feelings. In this way, not only are terms such as 'listening' introduced, but the effects of poor and good listening are illus-trated. Follow-up activities are provided to help the children use the skills effectively in a group and the programme also includes suggestions for generalising learnt skills.

Living Language by Ann Locke

This programme was designed for children who are finding it difficult to develop language spontaneously. It uses assessment procedures to iden-tify particular behaviours or aspects of language on which to focus when teaching and provides forms to record what has been learnt. The pro-gramme attempts to foster 'living language' by teaching in context, through everyday activities that involve interaction. It has three main sec-tions:

1. *Before Words* (for 'pre-language' children)
   The first section is widely used, as many other language pro-grammes do not cover this pre-verbal stage in such detail. It covers the four areas that underlie the emergence of understanding and the use of speech:
   • social and emotional development;
   • play;
   • listening;
   • expressive skills.
   Each area has six stages presented in developmental order. Each stage lists entry behaviours, which the child should exhibit before working on this stage, and target behaviours for teaching and asso-ciated behaviours, which often occur at the same time as the target behaviour. For example, one of the entry behaviours for 'manipula-tive exploratory play' is 'child pulls object towards himself' and the target behaviour is 'child looks for hidden object'.
       The clear layout of the stages makes it possible for the user to observe the child carefully and select target behaviours for each of

the four areas of pre-verbal development. Once a target behaviour is selected, suggested teaching strategies can be applied. For example, if the target behaviour is 'child looks for hidden object' then the adult can motivate the child by using an object the child likes, hide this object with a cover, use repeated demonstrations of pulling off the cover in an exaggerated way and use an exaggerated response when the object is uncovered. Eventually the child can be physically prompted to remove the cover if necessary and rewarded when he/she has done so.

2. *First Words* (for children with a limited vocabulary of mainly single words)

This part of the programme covers 100 words commonly occurring in early language development. The programme includes procedures to help the user select words to target. The teaching involves encouraging the children to use known words and expanding their utterances. For example, if the child says, 'gone', the adult might say, 'yes, your milk has gone'.

New words are taught by relating them first to tangible, familiar objects and events and then to other situations. The children initially become familiar with new words by hearing them used repeatedly in different contexts. They are then encouraged to demonstrate understanding of the words and, at the final stage, to use them.

3. *Putting Words Together* (for children who have a basic vocabulary and are starting to put words together)

This last section is intended to cover most of the remainder of language development. It covers a huge number of vocabulary items, including items that express properties and relationships, and a range of grammatical structures. The items are laid out in developmental order and the procedures outlined allow the user to select words and structures for teaching. Teaching procedures are similar to those used in the previous section and mainly involve using the targeted words and structures repeatedly in everyday contexts, including different areas of the school curriculum and topic work.

Teaching Talking by Ann Locke and Maggie Beech

The aim of this programme is to assist teachers working in mainstream nursery and primary schools to identify and manage children who are experiencing difficulty in acquiring spoken language. The 'teaching' mainly involves modifying the learning environment in order to give more focus to procedures and strategies that normally promote language development. The three stages of the programme (nursery, infant and junior) each provide an initial screening system, educational approaches, ways of recording progress and ideas and materials for working in more depth with children with significant difficulties.

The programme includes many useful detailed developmental charts and checklists such as the different uses of language that children acquire at preschool level, at infant level and at junior level. The record sheets provide details of specific skills expected at different stages of social-emotional development, intellectual development/play, listening/understanding and expressive skills.

Some general intervention strategies are suggested for children identified by the screening procedures. Examples include an allocated member of staff having a 'relaxed chat' with the child at least once a day and using the child's name to gain their attention before speaking to them.

Other intervention strategies are classified according to the difficulties experienced by the child. For example, with children who do not appear to listen to or understand spoken language, there are suggestions for supplementing spoken instructions with visual cues and ideas for checking that the child has understood.

If further assessment shows a significant language delay, further actions are suggested depending on the nature and degree of the delay. These include referrals to other professionals and suggestions for small group work with an adult and ideas on how to select children for the groups and how to record their progress. Behaviours listed on these progress charts provided are so specific that they also serve as targets for teaching.

Through monitoring the children's progress for three to four months it is possible to identify children who are making little or no progress in spoken language. Detailed profiles can then be used to guide further action such as referral to an educational psychologist. The profiles also identify specific behaviours that can be targeted more frequently either in a group or individually in the school.

A teaching resources handbook includes many ideas and activities that can be used in the classroom. For example, there is a section on 'activities to promote questioning' that includes the following ideas: For younger children – bringing in an interesting or unusual object, putting it in a secret box and then encouraging the children to ask questions to discover the identity. For older children – writing the names of famous people, television programmes, animals, plants on pieces of paper, pinning them on the children's backs and then telling the children to ask each other questions to discover who or what they are.

The Derbyshire Language Scheme by Wendy Knowles and Mark Masidlover

This programme was originally designed for children with severe learning disabilities. Therefore the complete programme includes a detailed 'progress record chart' that can be used with individual children, on which small steps in language development can be recorded and targeted. This chart is like a syllabus of normal language development and details language structures that are acquired at ten different levels. Although age-related stages are provided for the different levels, age equivalency is discouraged in the scheme.

The scheme includes an initial assessment procedure that enables the user to record the child's abilities on the progress record chart. Professionals are then advised to use the chart to plan teaching activities and record progress. All the language structures on the chart are cross-referenced to activities and teaching ideas in the two large teaching manuals.

For example, one of the structures on the chart at level 5 is *'using what + do'*. One of the corresponding teaching ideas for this structure includes making a toy teddy carry out various actions, such as packing a bag and laying out cups. The teacher tells the child to ask the teddy what he is doing.

To purchase the scheme the user has to attend an official three-day workshop. The programme and its training workshops introduced the concept of 'information carrying words' (ICW) to many members of the teaching and speech and language therapy professions in the UK. This concept is now widely used by many professionals.

ICWs refer to the number of words a child has to understand in order to carry out a request successfully. If a child is presented with a sponge and teddy that are familiar objects to him and asked to 'wash teddy' then this command has no information carrying words as the child can carry out the request through guesswork. However, if the child is presented with a brush and a sponge, and a doll and a teddy, then the same request has two information carrying words ('wash' and 'teddy'). The child has to distinguish between the uses of the sponge and the brush, as well as between the doll and the teddy.

In the manual the technique of focused stimulation is used. That is, repeating the targeted language structures in context so that the child will have many opportunities to link the structures with their meaning. The main aim of the teaching activities is to follow the principles of adapting everyday activities, ensuring that they are enjoyable and meaningful.

Chapter 9

Encouraging Language Development

Myra Kersner and Jannet A. Wright

The aim of any language work with children with communication problems is to help children attain a more acceptable level of language and communication skills for their age. Many of the examples given in this chapter refer to working in the classroom in a nursery or school, but playgroup workers or parents at home can also carry out the activities discussed. It is important for anyone working or playing with such children that they encourage language development as part of daily routines and in naturalistic settings.

Once children have been identified as having communication difficulties, it is useful to draw up a detailed description of what they can – as well as what they cannot – do in their daily lives. This may be particularly useful in helping to design a programme that may then be used specifically for an individual child. Children's behaviour in nursery or school, their performance in physical and social activities, as well as their school work should all be noted as these will contribute to a clearer picture of their abilities.

Nursery nurses, assistants and teachers have a number of important roles to play when faced with children with communication difficulties. They may have identified problems while working with the children or noted their behaviour in the classroom. Teachers and assistants may be the key people who are involved in implementing strategies and programmes, as well as providing a more sensitive environment for encouraging language development. Also, they may be called upon to monitor whether the children are using their new knowledge in the classroom setting.

How these roles are performed will be influenced by how the education staff view language; what they consider to be the stages of normal language development, and how they think language is acquired. The speech and language therapist will provide direction and support, but the education staff can ensure that children make maximum progress by providing them with optimum conditions and opportunities for encouraging communication.

Activities to encourage language

Each child is unique. Children with a language problem will require strategies tailored to meet their individual difficulties, needs and interests. In addition, they need to experience normal class activities and conversations. It should be possible to combine the two. Language programmes can be supplemented by classroom activities that encourage conversation in the class and develop underlying language skills.

It may be useful and time saving to collect and store in a box activities that have been enjoyed by the children. This may include some commercially available material as well as activities devised by the staff. For example, these could include games that:

- develop a child's knowledge of the world in specific areas such as colours and size;
- help a child to listen to spoken commands;
- help a child to remember spoken commands;
- help a child follow a short story.

The child's particular language ability will influence the choice of activity. The activities could be organised according to level of difficulty. Thus, easier tasks would be introduced first and harder ones presented only when the child has the necessary skills to progress.

For example, when listening to speech sounds it is easier for a child to distinguish between large differences in sounds and words, such as the difference between 'coat' and 'letter', before moving on to the harder task of choosing between words which sound very similar, such as 'coat' and 'goat'.

It is hard to hear the difference between two words that differ in only one sound. These are minimal pairs as referred to in Chapter 4. 'Car' and 'tar' are a minimal pair – the two words differ by only one sound.

So, when pictures are presented where the two words which the child has to choose between sound completely different, as in 'coat – letter', and the adult says: 'Show me the coat', it is comparatively easy for the child to pick out the word 'coat'. The task is harder if the adult says, 'Show me the coat', and the pair of words that the child has to choose between is 'coat – goat'. If the child cannot pick out the word 'coat' when paired with 'letter' it is unlikely that she or he would be able to pick out the word 'coat' from the pair 'coat – goat'.

Language tasks may be presented in picture, spoken or written form. Sometimes use can be made of books, commercial materials, toys, computer graphics and everyday objects, so long as the message is clear and a child's interest is captured.

Choosing the right level

Some activities are more complex than others, either because a high level of skill is required, or a number of different skills are involved in one activity. For example, if a child is told to 'Wash the doll's face', this involves at least three different levels of skill. In order to carry out this instruction, the child has to be able to:

1. listen to the speaker;
2. identify and remember the words;
3. carry out the task by picking up the doll and washing its face.

The number of skills required to complete a task must be considered. For example, children may find it difficult to build something while following the teacher's instructions, as they have to divide their attention between the speaker and the task. When asked to complete such a task, children who have poor hand control will find it even more difficult, as they are less able to give their full attention to the instructions. It may be easier for them if the instructions were split up into small chunks, the first given before they begin to build. Further instructions should be given only when the teacher has the child's full attention.

It is important to look carefully at the skills needed by children in any activity. They need to have the skills to achieve each stage of the activity if they are to succeed with the whole task.

What might appear to be a simple task to an adult may rely on skills which are developed over the years and which are performed almost automatically. For example, a popular activity when helping children to improve their attention and listening skills is to match a sound to a picture. A ball may be matched to the sound /b/ and a tap may be matched to the sound /t/. This matching can be done for all the sounds of English. Children may be given several picture cards, for example, of taps and balls. When they hear an adult make a sound such as /b/ or /t/ they are expected to identify an appropriate picture.

This may be an easy task for an adult but young children will find it more difficult. Adults may approach this task in two ways.

1. Learn by heart the sounds that are associated with each picture.
2. Use the learned ability to separate the sounds in the word (phonic skills) into /t–a–p/ to work out that the letter being represented by the picture 'tap' is /t/.

Young children are less able to do this task than adults, as they have fewer resources available. They are unlikely to have phonic skills, which are associated with reading; also their ability to remember information is limited. Thus the child's failure to perform the task may be due to limited memory, rather than inability to distinguish between sounds.

Language programmes

The term **language programme** is frequently used by professionals involved in working with children with communication difficulties. And yet each professional may use it in a different way. For example, there are the formalised published programmes such as those referred to in Chapter 8, and there are informal language programmes that are speech and language work schedules designed for individual children. The term language programme may refer to any structured framework that has been devised for the specific purpose of encouraging and teaching speech and language based on the careful assessment of individual children.

Any language programme should include the identification of language areas that need work and the specification of how this work may be fitted into the child's daily routine. Ideally the language areas, and specific items selected within them, should have maximum impact on the child's ability to influence and understand those around them.

For example, in the case of a non-verbal child it may be advisable not to teach long lists of 'things' or object names (nouns). If a smaller selection of these were taught together with a number of 'event' or 'action' words (verbs), such as 'do, go, make, be' the child would be able to combine two or more words to make simple sentences such as 'Mummy go;' 'Need drink;' 'Mummy make drink.'

It is important that the content of the activities and the way they are introduced should be adapted to each child's language level. Encouragement of language should not be restricted to set times and set tasks. Although it may be important to set aside special sessions in order to work on some more formalised language programmes, as discussed in Chapter 8, it must be remembered that in order for language work to be beneficial it needs to become part of, and have an effect on, the child's daily routine.

There may be some skill areas such as attention and listening that require specific work that may necessitate the child being withdrawn from the classroom or group activity. However, even these skills will need to become part of the children's daily experiences if they are to have an influence on their ability to communicate.

Ways of responding

Children's levels of functioning are affected by the way in which adults respond to and communicate with them. Often in a classroom setting a conversation between a teacher and a child will be one-sided, with the teacher doing all the talking.

Teachers who want to try and change this pattern could listen to a tape of themselves talking to the children or ask a colleague to write down what they say. This may help them to gain insight into the way they talk and listen in a conversation.

If time can be found, consistently, for one adult to play with and talk to a child, communication is likely to become more rewarding. By communicating one-to-one with the same person the child may gain confidence. It will provide opportunities for both the adult and child to adapt to one another's behaviour and style of speaking.

When adults are talking to children, especially children with language difficulties, they need to limit what they say, slow their speech down and leave longer than normal pauses between turns so that children have time to understand what has been said, and put together a reply. Adults may have to start the conversation that will, ideally, arise from an activity or object that holds the attention of both the adult and the child. Then, adults will encourage the exchange of ideas by prompting the child to communicate again.

However, the contributions made to the conversation should be balanced, so the child must be encouraged or allowed to take the lead at times. Children need the opportunity to introduce topics for conversation, ask questions and respond to questions, as soon as they are able. Children are less likely to contribute if the adults continually adopt a controlling role and ask a great number of questions. This situation can arise when adults are busy, especially if children appear to offer little, or their contributions are unintelligible. As children's language develops and they practise using their new skills it should be easier to have a conversation with them and to see them as equal partners.

It should be remembered that even children who have difficulty with words are still capable of communicating. Responses should be made to any attempts at communication that for some children might involve gaze direction, hand pointing, body position and occasional vocalisations instead of words. These cues often are unclear and may be misinterpreted at times, but at least they give some idea of the child's interests and desire to communicate. Adults will need to use non-verbal responses such as gesture and facial expression, to support their speech when responding to such children.

How to ensure progress

The aim of encouraging language development is to enable children to use their communication skills to have an effect on the environment. For example, if they want a drink they can ask for some juice. Learning lists of words, phrases and sentences may not be helpful as they are unlikely to be used outside the taught situation.

Children acquire language by identifying the rules that operate in their language from the examples presented to them, and from these make their own sentences that can be used in new situations. Children may overuse certain new rules as explained in Chapter 2, but it is important to recognise this as a part of the learning process. Clear examples and repetition of the same situations increase the likelihood of connections being made between the words and the grammatical rules.

If children are to acquire and use language they hear within the class in new situations, then it must reflect the language of their environment. They need to acquire conversational English. For example, if a child is shown a picture of a woman cooking and asked what the woman is doing, the most acceptable response would be 'cooking' rather than a full sentence.

Modelling

As explained in Chapter 2, modelling occurs spontaneously with children when they are acquiring language. If a child is having difficulties learning to talk, then this strategy of modelling may be used to improve and extend what the child says. Thus, the listener uses the child's utterance and takes it one stage further, using the same form but adding to its length and complexity. This is demonstrated in the example below.

> Child: 'Cat eat.'
> Adult: 'The cat is eating.'
> Child: 'Cat eating.'
> Adult: 'The cat is eating some fish.'

It may be possible to use modelling to create a new sentence while maintaining the topic as in the next example.

> Child: 'The man is shopping.'
> Adult: 'Yes, he has bought a shirt.'
> Child: 'Look, money.'
> Adult: 'He will have to give the lady some money for the shirt.'

Questions to children

Every effort should be made to use language to convey an appropriate message. It is best to avoid asking children **display questions**, where the child knows that the speaker already has the answer. For example, a mother might ask 'What colour pencil is this?' but the child realises that the mother knows the answer because she is looking at the pencil. It would be more appropriate for the mother to ask the same question when only the child can see the object and she cannot.

Wood *et al.* (1990) state that questions by their very nature are controlling and demanding. They found that if questions are asked in the classroom, the children answer the questions, but say little else. Also, the children made more contributions and longer utterances when there were fewer questions in the conversation. Children may be encouraged to make more contributions if teachers talk about their own experiences and/or comment on what the child has to offer.

However, it is natural to ask questions, and some will be needed to ensure that the conversation is not incomprehensible. Questions are more successful if they relate to the theme or contribution a child has already made.

Questions that begin with 'Where?', 'What?', 'Why?' or 'When?' may help clarify a topic of conversation. However, children will need to understand the concepts of time and place in order to answer questions beginning with 'When', 'What' or 'Where' and they will need to have a conceptual understanding of cause and effect before they can answer 'Why?' or 'How?' questions. Such questions are more likely to get an appropriate response if the children understand the relevance of the particular question word (see Chapter 2).

If a child does not respond to questions then **two-choice** or **forced-alternatives** may be used. For example: 'Are you happy or sad today?' and 'Would you like milk or juice?'

Feedback

In order that children progress, it is necessary for them to know whether they have been successful in their attempts at communication. They need to know if they have successfully conveyed their message and that they have been understood. Most of the time it is appropriate to tell them so.

The natural way that adult listeners can indicate that the child's message has been successfully conveyed is by doing what is asked, or by continuing the conversation by expanding the topic being discussed. If children's messages are incomplete then an incorrect action or reply will let them know this.

Adults may help children to produce a clearer message by stating that their message was unclear, or seeking confirmation by asking them: 'Do you mean X or Y?' It is more difficult to communicate with a child whose speech is unintelligible as guesswork may be needed to aid interpretation.

If children fail to understand what they are being told or asked to do, then the message may need to be restated more simply. Requests may be repeated so that children have a second attempt at understanding what was said. Or, they may be broken down into simple stages, thereby reducing the length of the instruction that needs to be held and understood at any one time.

As a last resort it may be possible to demonstrate the request. Altering what is said or increasing the amount of information in the instruction is likely to confuse more than assist the child.

How to monitor progress

Keeping a record of developing skills and monitoring progress is essential to ensure that genuine improvement is being made by the child. This information will help to establish whether easier communication is a result of an improvement in the adult's ability to interpret the child's speech, or whether what the child says, and how she or he says it has altered. These records also should highlight any change, particularly in children with multiple problems or behavioural difficulties, where progress is slow or often not recognised. This will prevent a child whose behaviour has improved from being unrecognised and unrewarded.

The records can take the form of tape recordings, video recordings, checklists, or written records of children's understanding and use of language. The method selected will be influenced by the time available for the task. The information collected will enable the staff to know whether the language and activities selected for the children are pitched at an appropriate level and whether they are ready to progress to the next goal.

What language should be encouraged

Children with language problems mainly use language when they need help, for example with 'toileting' or feeding. Attempts at giving information and making social contacts are often limited. Opportunities for using language in this way are more likely to occur in situations of significance to the child, such as discussion of current and home events or future outings. The content of the conversations will depend on the child's language skills. The adult will take the lead in putting words to actions, introducing new vocabulary, or increasing the complexity of a child's utterances. Introduction of new materials needs to be controlled, so that there is recognisable order and progress can be noted. New words or ideas should be incorporated into the child's existing knowledge of language and the world.

Children with language difficulties may need an environment that is organised and full of opportunities to hear and use language, but non-stop talking to them is not the answer. Short, regular sessions during which language is specifically encouraged, which build up the child's abilities gradually, are more likely to be successful and rewarding to both parties. Children are likely to tire quickly in tasks that require them to use their weaker skills and after a while they may switch off or opt out.

Who should encourage language?

In order to give children the best chance of improving their communication skills the social and physical environments need to be considered as well as the content of the interaction. Children with language difficulties are a varied group. Some may be quiet and withdrawn, while others are loud and difficult to manage. All are likely to have impaired contact with their environment.

Activities such as play, which use the same skills as language, may be delayed. Play provides children with the opportunity to understand their world, to work with others, and to use their language. Children with communication problems may have difficulties starting and developing their play, which may be repetitive and solitary. They may stand and watch other children playing together, but lack the skills required to become involved with another child. Limited play and language skills are likely to result in difficulties interacting with other children.

For children with language problems, support and practice of their communication skills is unlikely to be provided by their peer group and they seldom use their language to form social contacts. Furthermore they are less able to have successful and prolonged conversations with their classmates. Even children who do not have communication problems have a great deal of linguistic knowledge to acquire before they are as mature as adults are in their communication. Thus they are unable, and possibly unwilling, to facilitate a child less able than themselves.

Children with language problems need the encouragement and the skills of the adults around them in order to help them develop their language. Initially the teacher, nursery nurse or assistant may interact with the child on his or her own. As confidence and language skills increase, a child may be encouraged to work with one other child, then in a small group before being expected to join in activities with larger groups of children. The adult's role in starting and maintaining the conversation can gradually be withdrawn.

The child with language difficulties needs a great deal of individual attention and will find group situations difficult to handle. Even young children with normally developing speech and language find it no easy matter to make themselves understood in a group setting.

However, as Reilly (2001) shows, some small group activities may be useful for encouraging language.

Where should language be encouraged?

Conversations for young children are likely to revolve around the happenings and social practices of their everyday life. Although it may be necessary sometimes to withdraw children from the classroom for specific language work, wherever and whenever possible language should be encouraged during their class activities. This will ensure that the language used with the children is useful and meaningful.

It may be possible to arrange the environment in order to:

* *Maximise the child's need to communicate.* For example, a wanted or needed object can be placed in a clear container with a lid that is difficult to remove, so that the child is more likely to request assistance.
* *Make the meanings of words more apparent.* For example, limit the number of options present as in the forced-alternative example given above. It may also be helpful to act on/do what the child has actually said to illustrate the meaning of the word that the child has used.

Many different opportunities can be provided to enable the child to discover the meanings of words and to use them in conversations. There are different situations where a word can occur, for example the word 'in'. This may appear in different contexts such as: shopping in the basket; washing in the machine; or juice in the cup.

A shared interest is necessary for communication, so the content of the discussion must be mutually agreed upon. Initially this should be directed by the children's interest, by what they are looking at or playing with in the class. An activity selected by the child is more likely to be maintained and, therefore, is the logical focus for conversation.

Different activities will influence the quantity and content of the language produced by the child. Construction tasks such as Lego are unlikely to provide the opportunities for extended conversations. Similarly if the child is running around they will be out of breath and more concerned with action than with words.

Bruner (1980) found that fantasy play in the 'home corner' and play with dolls were more likely to encourage verbal exchanges. His study also found that children said more in these environments when adults were not involved. However, as discussed earlier, language disordered children need the support of an adult in order to initiate and maintain the conversation.

Conclusion

Children with language problems are best helped by those who are interested in working with them. Positive improvement in a child's language development will be encouraged by educational staff who are able to spend time with the child. They are in a position to provide the naturalistic setting in which children's language skills may develop. Although the children's progress may be gradual and continue throughout their time in school, with interest and enthusiasm from the staff combined with an understanding of language, the children may achieve their full potential.

Further reading

Cooke, J. and Williams, D. (1991) *Working with Children's Language*, 2nd edn. Bicester: Winslow Press/Speechmark.
Delamain, C. and Spring, J. (2000) *Developing Baseline Communication Skills.* Bicester: Winslow Press/Speechmark.

Chapter 10

Working with Parents
Monica Bray

Sure Start: Making a difference for children and families (DfEE 1999) puts parents and families at the centre of the wheel of support for children. It also shows how collaboration between parents and agencies that provide child care and education is essential for the child's well-being. Government papers such as this and *Excellence for All Children: Meeting special educational needs* (DfEE 1997) demonstrate how the importance and necessity of working with parents is embedded in government policy.

Professionals need to realise that there are numerous layers of information and support for parents provided by others and that their place in the relationship with the child may be far from central. To work well in collaboration with parents will require a special awareness and/or relationships with all the involved others. This can be seen in the model in Figure 10.1.

The particular concern of this chapter is the relationship between the professional and the parents, but it is important to bear in mind that the child is at the centre of this whole system and there may be many influences on the parents from various layers of the system. If the relationship between parents and professional is going to be truly collaborative, it is the professional's duty to try to understand what the parents' feelings, knowledge and beliefs are and how they have come about.

How might children's difficulties affect parents?

Self-blame, guilt, pain and anger, frustration, disappointment, sadness, helplessness, annoyance and worry: these are some of the feelings expressed by parents of children who stammer during a group therapy session. And it is not only children who stammer who raise these feelings in their parents. Parents of children who have speech and language delay have also expressed feelings of inadequacy, not knowing where to turn to next, frustration at being unable to help their children, guilt and anger.

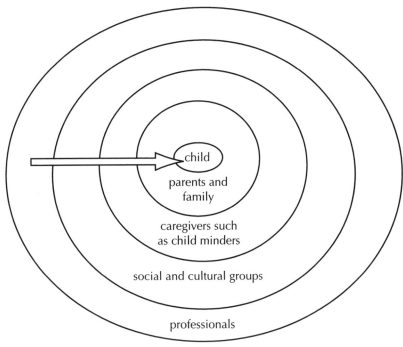

Figure 10.1 Relationships between parents, professionals and children

Most parents who find out that their child has problems and is not developing as expected will react with concern (What does this mean for my child?), and often guilt (What have I done wrong?) or anger (What has gone wrong? Who is to blame?). There may be differences in the ways that mothers and fathers react which can cause additional conflict (Burgess 1997). Parents with a child who is not developing speech, fluency or language find themselves at a loss. They can no longer apply the rules of child rearing that have worked before in this family or in this culture. Many parents will describe such feelings as: .

- **denial** that the problem exists which may lead to a never-ending search to find someone who will simply 'cure' it;
- **anger** which is directed at a range of people, professionals included, who may be seen as not doing enough to help the child overcome the difficulty;
- **depression** as they become aware of the inevitability of the condition (it is not just going to disappear overnight), leading them to feeling inadequate and unable to cope with the difficulties facing them;

- **acceptance** which for some people is helpful and leads to being able to become involved in helping the child as much as is possible, but on the other hand can lead to 'giving up' and simply letting nature take its course.

(Lendrum and Syme 1992)

Of course, many families cope extremely well and have few of these feelings. We should never assume that dealing with a child with difficulties is going to be a negative experience for all.

However, the fact remains that this child will be different in some ways from other children that the parent knows. The process of speech and language development usually occurs without parents doing anything specific. The child will 'pick up' language from just being exposed to normal daily routines, unlike toilet training, for example, where a parent has a definite teaching role. So, when language and speech are not developing, parents will not automatically know what to do. They are likely to have no common-sense knowledge about the way in which their own speech and language behaviour might help or hinder their child's development. They may feel unskilled and useless.

Parents are likely to turn to their families and their social or cultural leaders to try to explain the child's problems. Myths and stories about child development will abound. Some of these may be very helpful and give the parents a sense of support, others may be quite destructive and undermine what the parents themselves feel would be best.

A helpful family myth: All the boys in our family are slow at starting to talk. Some of them just grew out of it and some needed a bit of help. They are all fine now.
An unhelpful family myth: Stammering is caused by nerves. Your uncle cured himself by taking a cold bath every day. That toughened him up.

Parents' child-rearing approaches will be driven by their own goals related to what they want from their children and what they want for their children (LeVin 1974 cited in Goodnow and Collins 1990: 18). Goodnow and Collins put forward evidence to show that what parents often want from their children are such things as:

- affection;
- stimulation and fun;
- social identity;
- economic support.

The parents also want their children to have access to a range of things that start with basic physical needs, such as survival and good health, and move up a hierarchy to certain culturally specific values, such as loyalty and honesty (see Figure 10.2).

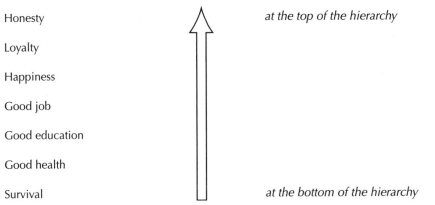

Honesty		*at the top of the hierarchy*
Loyalty		
Happiness		
Good job		
Good education		
Good health		
Survival		*at the bottom of the hierarchy*

Figure 10.2 Hierarchy of things parents want for their children

If the developmental delay that the child is experiencing impacts on any of the particular values and goals of parents, they will obviously be disturbed and upset by the child's problems.

What do parents need to help them deal with their child?

As a professional if you think about your own situation where something is not going well and you feel unable to deal with it, what are your needs? Probably you need:

- information and knowledge of the problem and the situation;
- support from someone who can help you decide what are possible ways forward;
- support from someone who you can talk to about how things are going;
- an understanding of what is possible and what is not possible so that you do not have false expectations of what you should be able to achieve;
- to have your views listened to and valued.

Parents are likely to have similar needs. But you should be aware of some of the pitfalls of trying to meet parents' needs (Table 10.1).

Table 10.1 Pitfalls of trying to meet parents' needs

Need to be met	What can get in the way
Information	Too much given. Wrong language code used – language level too high or low, mother tongue not used. Parents are too upset to absorb it.
Knowledge	Level of background knowledge not assessed so too high or too low a level assumed. Patronising parents by telling them what they already know.
Support	Too many different professionals trying to offer support. Not accepting the amount of support that parents can gain from friends or selves. Trying to intervene too much.
Working out what is possible	Not starting from what the parent knows or believes. Not assuming the same values, expectations and goals.
Listening	Telling parents what to do instead of listening to what they already do. Not listening to what the meaning behind the words may be.

Values, knowledge and skills held by the professional

Values, beliefs or attitudes

Values, beliefs or attitudes that are held by you will be a major influence on your work with parents. There are a number of issues that you need to consider.

What are your beliefs and values about family systems and parenting? Parenting in this country may no longer reflect the images we still see on television or read about in books. The four-person family with father as head and breadwinner and mother as primary carer and houseparent has long gone. Different family patterns such as single parent families, parents of the same sex, extended families, families where one or both parents work away from home, reconstituted families with children from different liaisons living in the home, and many more variations, are becoming the norm in Britain as a multicultural and non-discriminatory society (Pugh *et al.*1994).

What behaviours do you expect to see in parents' relationships with their children? Parental roles of caring, playing, instructing, admonishing and administering punishment are also changing and there is no easily identifiable 'norm' or set of behaviours that can be used as a guideline. Each family, each parent and each child is unique and a unique way of dealing with the issues that may be a problem needs to be found.

What were the goals of having children in your family? The way in which your family and culture define children and childhood will have been implanted into your way of thinking. Is the child seen as 'an imp or an angel'? Is he or she born with 'original sin or original innocence'? Does the child need to be allowed to grow freely or to be shaped into an expected moral form? (Goodnow and Collins, 1990: 22).

Think about some of these questions.

- What was my own upbringing like?
- Who was the main caregiver in my family?
- What was the approach to child rearing when I was young?
- What were the expectations in relation to behaviour, play and education?
- Do I still believe what my parents believed?
- How have I changed and why?
- How strong are my beliefs – do I carry a set of 'commands' in my head? such as 'Honour thy father and mother, do not steal, children should be seen and not heard'.
- What are my views on how much or how little a parent should talk to his or her child?
- How much should the child be read to?
- How important is communication between family members?

The important thing to consider is – how do this parent and child differ from your own experience? Are you likely to let your own background and beliefs affect the way in which you view and understand parents you may work with? It is important to be aware of your own capacity to feel, your anxieties and sense of worth and your motives for wanting to work with children and parents (Nelson-Jones 1997).

Knowledge

Having completed a self-evaluation, it is now important to move on to think about your own knowledge base and need for more knowledge. What do you know about:

- this parent, this child, this family?
- the beliefs and values the parents come with?
- the cultural and societal influences on the situation?
- the economic pressures the parents are dealing with?
- the level of knowledge the parent has in relation to the child's speech and language difficulties?
- the speech and language used in this family?

Also what knowledge do you have about:

- speech and language development and what influences it?
- children's play and interaction?
- children's capacity for learning?
- adult learning styles?
- how to form and work with groups?
- why people behave and relate the way they do?
- why mothers and fathers may behave differently?

Think also about where you can obtain this knowledge. Can you find out directly from the parents? Can you find out from members of the community; from self-help groups; from pamphlets and information packs; from academic books; from short courses; or from special interest groups? There are numerous ways to obtain information and often it is most useful to gather ideas from a wide range of sources rather than just from one. For example, parent comment is very relevant but by its nature very personal, while academic literature is likely to be objective and highly regarded but possibly not valid for the situation in which you find yourself.

Skills

Finally, you need to consider what you can actually do for this parent. What you can do will relate to the parent and child's needs; the present circumstances in relation to health and welfare currently experienced by the family; the setting in which you may see the child and parents; the resources available in terms of time and materials, space and transport; intellectual and emotional levels of the parents; and the managerial structures and pressures put upon you. You cannot apply a 'cookbook' approach to all families. Each family, each parent, each child, each situation is unique. There are useful parent-based programmes in the literature (ways of managing behaviour, teaching a child to read or helping the child develop a speech sound system) that can be used for support, but none of these can be applied indiscriminately to all families. Parents can feel undervalued if the professional simply gives them a printed sheet from a manual. One parent I knew refused to accept that her child could be anything like other children – so how could this general information apply to her!

Some of the skills you need to develop in order to be effective in your work with parents are described here.

Basic counselling skills. Burnard (1994) believes all those who work with people should have these. They are based on the 'core conditions' described by Carl Rogers (1951) and are seen as being necessary for any good relationship.

- **Genuineness and honesty**: do not pretend to be what you are not or to know what you do not know; relate to the parent with genuine interest and concern for the welfare of both the parent and the child.
- **Non-judgemental attitude**: do not judge people's behaviour by your own standards, find out why they are acting the way they do; accept people for what they are.
- **Empathy or understanding**: try to imagine what it must be like to be this parent managing these problems; try to understand what the parent feels and how this affects the way he or she acts towards the child.

Problem-solving and decision-making skills. These are based on an understanding of how you learn, enabling you to work with the parent to break down the problems and tasks into small steps and attempt to change one step at a time. They also relate to setting up strategies with the parent for coping with difficult times and dealing with problems of behaviour.

Teaching skills. These will be needed when specific tasks need to be described and demonstrated to parents.

Leadership skills. These will be necessary when you are running groups for parents.

Some ways of working with parents

It is important to think carefully about what might be best for a parent and child. Some of the variations in how you might approach work with parents and the consequences of your decisions are considered here.

Where to work?

Should you see the parent in the clinic, in the child's nursery or school, in the parent's home or in an educational or family centre? Being flexible and offering appointments as far as possible that suit the life styles of the parents is essential. Table 10.2 shows a number of factors that might help you decide where to work.

Table 10.2 Factors to consider when deciding where to work

Context	Positive aspects	Negative aspects
Clinic	You feel comfortable here. You can prepare toys and furnishings to suit you. All your equipment is to hand. It is quiet and private.	The parent may connect the clinic with a medical model of 'cure'. The parent and child may be overwhelmed by the setting and be unable to communicate well. It may be difficult to get to and travel may be too expensive. The hours of opening may be inappropriate for the family. There may be cultural issues (woman unable to travel without husband) that reduce attendance.
Nursery or school	Many of the professionals who see this child are available. The child and parent are familiar with the setting and with the materials and equipment. The child may play or behave more naturally as other children are around. The parent is likely to be dropping off or picking up the child so does not have to make a special journey.	There may be no privacy for the parent. The environment may be noisy and distracting for the parent and child. There may be no special place to sit and talk. If you are a visiting professional, you may not be able to choose your date or time.

Table 10.2 continued

Context	Positive aspects	Negative aspects
Parental home	The parent is in control and so may feel less threatened. The child will be at home and more comfortable. You will be aware of the availability of toys, books and space for the child. The relationship is likely to be more relaxed and less formal.	You have to spend time travelling and you need to carry resources with you. It can be threatening to the professional to be in someone else's home. There may be distractions from other family members, visitors, telephone, television or video.
Education or family centre	Neutral ground can often be a comfortable place to be. Room size and availability may be good – especially for groups. Additional resources such as a library or computers may be available.	It may be threatening to some families. It may be impersonal and uncomfortable. Special equipment may not be available.

Who to work with?

Encouraging both parents to be involved, welcoming other children into the clinic, asking extended family members or friends to attend with the child and parent can all make for a more relaxed and friendly atmosphere. It can also give the professional a much better idea of how the child interacts with others and how the family manages the difficulties of the child.

Encouraging groups of parents to get together for discussion and mutual support or bringing groups of parents and their children together to learn and play can be an excellent way for information and skills to be imparted without pressure from the professional. Parents are very good at sharing practical ideas of ways forward. A parent is much more likely to accept ideas and information from another parent than from a professional. Running a therapy group where the aims are for parents to express their worries and concerns can enable parents to change attitudes and move towards a positive acceptance of the child's problems. Seeing that others share similar concerns is an excellent way for parents to feel less isolated and more supported.

An 'open' clinic can be a useful idea. Parents can drop in at any time between set parameters which allows the choice of when to attend to be made by them so reducing the pressure of keeping a formal appointment which might be difficult for people from cultures where time is not so 'precious' as it is in White British culture. When other children are present, such as younger siblings or others attending the clinic, the play situation is more natural and the therapist can get a more realistic picture of the child.

What to do?

1. *Giving the power to the parents.* The power in a professional–parent relationship is biased towards the professional and it is all too easy to reinforce this by playing the part of the 'expert' or the teacher. Cunningham and Davis (1985) give some useful advice about how to reflect on the nature of your relationship with parents. You need to be self-aware and sensitive to the parents and accept their expertise with their child in order to avoid being in the power position. You also need to ask them what they want and work with their concerns, not the other way around. Remember that parents are the experts regarding their own children.

2. *Improving parent–child communication.* Your main aim is to enable the parent and child to communicate effectively in whatever way is best for them. This may mean informing the parent about such things as the importance of non-verbal communication, responsiveness to the child, observing the child's style of learning and the importance of play. There is no better way of proving the usefulness of an approach than demonstrating it and having the parent try it out there and then. This can be less threatening if there is a group of parents and children working together. Be aware though that there is a fine balance between helping a parent to communicate more effectively with the child and disturbing their natural communication and making the parent feel awkward and de-skilled.

3. *Supporting the parent through change.* When a child has a speech or language difficulty, parents may be asked to change the way in which they might naturally behave with their child. Change is difficult and maintaining new skills is even harder. Parents may feel abandoned if they are given one session or a list of 'dos and don'ts' and are then not seen for many months. Keeping in touch is essential, face-to-face, through email or by telephone.

Finally

Professionals can be both helpful and threatening. You need to be aware of how much pressure your involvement may place on a family. This is particularly an issue with vulnerable families. Booth and Booth (1994) have shown that families in which one of the parents has a learning difficulty feel overwhelmed. Professionals take up time, often give conflicting advice and may be seen as the instrument of the state who might take the child away. As a professional you must show that you respect the parent and child bond, must offer consistent and non-intrusive support, must work in small steps and not overwhelm parents. Sometimes you need to realise that therapy for the child is not appropriate at this point as there are more pressing difficulties for the family, such as bereavement, illness, financial difficulties or housing problems. Failure to attend clinic appointments does not signify a lack of concern for the child. Such failure may be due to some of the factors described above, or there may be a difference of opinion between the professional and the parents in relation to the severity of the child's speech and language problem. Different cultural expectations for development and different levels of involvement and intervention in children's development are also likely to make for different levels of commitment from the families.

Working with parents is not an easy option. It requires time, knowledge, special skills and a belief in the necessity of sharing knowledge and of learning from parents about their children. Confident and happy children require confident and happy parents (Pugh *et al.* 1994) and you may have the privilege of being of some help in achieving this.

Further reading

Goodnow, J. and Collins, W. (1990) *Development According to Parents: The nature, sources and consequences of parents' ideas.* Hove: Lawrence Erlbaum Associates.

Pugh, G., De'Ath, E. and Smith, C. (1994) *Confident Parents, Confident Children: Policy and practice in parent education and support.* London: National Children's Bureau.

Whalley, M. and The Pen Green Centre Team (1997) *Working with Parents.* London: Hodder and Stoughton.

Glossary

BLISSYMBOLS: This is a structured system – with its own grammar – of diagrammatic symbols that represent spoken words. The symbol elements are put together in different combinations and are repeated with consistent meaning. It is used most widely by people with physical disabilities to help them to communicate.

BRITISH SIGN LANGUAGE (BSL): The sign language used by many deaf people in Britain. It does not follow the same word order as spoken English, but has a grammar and structure of its own.

CEREBRAL PALSY: Brain damage that may occur before, during or shortly after birth. Children with cerebral palsy usually have some degree of physical disability, which may affect vocal communication. In some cases children may also have learning disabilities.

CLEFT LIP and/or PALATE: A structural abnormality that affects the developing foetus and is present at birth. It involves the hard palate and/or soft palate (roof of the mouth) that fail to meet completely. It may be associated with a cleft lip. Both conditions are normally treated surgically and treatment may continue until a child is in his/her late teens. In babies and young children there may be feeding difficulties, and some articulation problems may occur.

ENGLISH AS AN ADDITIONAL LANGUAGE (EAL): Refers to children for whom English is not the language spoken in the home. They learn, and often use, English as an additional language.

LEARNING DISABILITIES: Refers to people who have some degree of cognitive difficulties. May also be referred to as 'mental handicap' or 'mental retardation'.

MAKATON SYMBOLS: A system of stylised pictures that are used to represent the signs of **MAKATON**. This refers to a system of 300 plus specific signs that have been specially selected from BSL. The symbols are widely used with people with learning disabilities to help them communicate.

References

Adams, M. R. (1977) 'A clinical strategy for differentiating the normal nonfluent child and the incipient stutterer', *Journal of Fluency Disorders* **2**, 141–8.

Andersen-Wood, L. and Rae Smith, B. (1997) *Working with Pragmatics.* Bicester: Winslow Press/Speechmark.

Andrews, G. and Harris, M. (1964) *The Syndrome of Stuttering.* London: The Spastics Society with Heinemann Medical Books.

Bloodstein, O. (1995) *A Handbook on Stuttering.* London: Chapman and Hall.

Booth, T. and Booth, W. (1994) *Parenting Under Pressure: Mothers and fathers with learning difficulties.* Milton Keynes: Open University Press.

Bruner, J. S. (1975) 'The ontogenesis of speech acts', *Journal of Child Language* **2**(1), 1–20.

Bruner, J. S. (1980) *Under Five in Britain.* Oxford Preschool Research Project: Grant McIntyre Ltd.

Burgess, A. (1997) *Fatherhood Reclaimed: The making of the modern father.* London: Vermilion Press.

Burnard, P. (1994) *Counselling Skills for Health Professionals*, 2nd edn. London: Chapman and Hall.

Chomsky, N. A. (1959) 'Review of verbal behaviour by B. F. Skinner', *Language* **35**, 26–58.

Christie, E. (2000) *The Primary Healthcare Workers' Project: A 4-year investigation into changing referral patterns to ensure the early identification and referral of dysfluent preschoolers in the UK.* London: The British Stammering Association.

Clarke, M., Price, K. and Jolleff, N. (2001) 'Augmentative and alternative communication', in Kersner, M. and Wright, J. A. (eds) *Speech and Language Therapy: The decision-making process when working with children*, 268–82. London: David Fulton Publishers.

Conture, E. G. and Caruso, A. J. (1987) 'Assessment and diagnosis of childhood dysfluency', in Rustin, L., Purser, H. and Rowley, D. (eds) *Progress in the Treatment of Fluency Disorders.* London: Taylor and Francis.

Cooke, J. and Williams, D. (1991) *Working with Children's Language*, 2nd edn. Bicester: Winslow Press/Speechmark.

Cooper, E. B. and Cooper, C. S. (1985) *Cooper Personalized Fluency Control Therapy*. (Revised edn) Allen, Texas: DLM Teaching Resources.

Crystal, D. (1986) *Listen to your Child: Parents' guide to children's language*. Harmondsworth: Penguin Books.

Cunningham, C. and Davis, H. (1985) *Working with Parents: Frameworks for collaboration*. Milton Keynes: Open University Press.

Davis, A. (1998) 'Performance of neonatal and infant hearing screens: sensitivity and specificity', in *European Consensus Statement on Neonatal Hearing Screening*. European Consensus Development Conference on Neonatal Hearing Screening, Milan, 15–16 May.

Delamain, C. and Spring, J. (2000) *Developing Baseline Communication Skills*. Bicester: Winslow Press/Speechmark.

DfEE (1997) *Excellence for All Children: Meeting special educational needs*. London: The Stationery Office.

DfEE (1999) *Sure Start: Making a difference for children and families*. London: The Stationery Office.

Effective Health Care Bulletin (1992) 'The treatment of persistent glue ear in children', *Effective Health Care Bulletin* **4**, 1–16.

Goodnow, J. and Collins, W. (1990) *Development According to Parents: The nature, sources and consequences of parents' ideas*. Hove: Lawrence Erlbaum Associates.

Graham, P., Turk, J. and Verhurst, F.C. (1999) *Child Psychiatry*, 3rd edn. Oxford: Oxford University Press.

Gregory, H. and Hill, D. (1993) 'Differential evaluation – differential therapy for stuttering children', in Curlee, R. (ed.) *Stuttering and Related Disorders of Fluency*, 23–44. New York: Thieme Medical Publishers Inc.

Herbert, M. (1996) *ABC of Behavioural Methods*. Leicester: The British Psychological Society Books.

Kidd, K. K., Kidd, J.R. and Records, M.A. (1978) 'The possible causes of the sex ratio in stuttering and its implications', *Journal of Fluency Disorders* **3**, 13–23.

Knowles, W. and Masidlover, M. (1982) *The Derbyshire Language Scheme*. Ripley: Derbyshire Education Authority.

Law, J. (ed.) (1992) *The Early Identification of Language Impairment in Children*. London: Chapman and Hall.

Lendrum, S. and Syme, G. (1992) *Gift of Tears: A practical approach to loss and bereavement counselling*. London: Routledge.

Locke, A. (1985) *Living Language*. Windsor: NFER Nelson.

Locke, A. and Beech, M. (1991) *Teaching Talking.* Windsor: NFER Nelson.

Lynch, C. and Kidd, J. (1999) *Early Communication Skills.* Bicester: Winslow Press/Speechmark.

McCormick, B. (1993) 'Behavioural hearing tests 6 months to 3.5 years', in McCormick, B. (ed.) *Paediatric Audiology 0–5 Years*, 2nd edn. London: Whurr Publishers Ltd, pp. 102–23.

Manolson, A. (1992) *It Takes Two to Talk.* Toronto: Hanen Centre.

Manolson, A., Ward, B. and Dodington, N. (1995) *You Make the Difference.* Toronto: The Hanen Centre.

Meyers, S. C. and Woodford, L. L. (1992) *The Fluency Development System.* Buffalo, New York: United Educational Services.

MorganBarry, R. A. (1988) *Auditory Discrimination and Attention Test.* Windsor: NFER-Nelson.

Murray, H. L. and Reed, C. G. (1977) 'Language abilities of pre-school stuttering children', *Journal of Fluency Disorders* **2**, 171–6.

National Institute for Clinical Excellence (NICE) www.nice.org.uk

Nelson-Jones, R. (1997) *Practical Counselling and Helping Skills*, 4th edn. London: Cassell.

Prizant, B. M. *et al.* (1990) 'Communication disorders and emotional/behavioural disorders in children and adolescents', *Journal of Speech and Hearing Disorders* **55**, 179–92.

Pugh, G., De'Ath, E. and Smith, C. (1994) *Confident Parents, Confident Children: Policy and practice in parent education and support.* London: National Children's Bureau.

Reilly, O. (2001) 'Managing children individually and in groups', in Kersner, M. and Wright, J. A. (eds) *Speech and Language Therapy: The decision-making process when working with children*, 40–52. London: David Fulton Publishers.

Richman, N., Stevenson, J. and Graham, P. (1982) *Pre-school to School: A behavioural study.* London: Academic Press.

Riley, G. (1981) *Stuttering Prediction Instrument for Young Children.* Austen: PRO-ED.

Riley, G. D. and Riley, J. A. (1984) 'A component model for treating stuttering in children', in Peins, M. (ed.) *Contemporary Approaches in Stuttering Therapy*, 123–71. Boston, USA: Little, Brown & Co.

Rinaldi, W. (1995) *Social Use of Language Programme for Primary and Infant School Children.* Windsor: NFER-Nelson.

Rogers, C. (1951) *Client-centered Therapy.* Boston: Houghton Mifflin.

Royal College of Speech and Language Therapists (RCSLT) (1996) *Communicating Quality 2.* London: RCSLT.

Rustin, L., Botterill, W. and Kelman, E. (1996) *Assessment and Therapy for Young Dysfluent Children.* London: Whurr Publishers.

Rutter, M., Cox, A., Tupling, C., Berger, M. and Yule, W. (1975) 'Attainment and adjustment in two geographical areas: prevalence of psychiatric disorders', *British Journal of Psychiatry* **126**, 493–509.

Sheehan, J. G. (ed.) (1970) *Stuttering Research and Therapy.* New York: Harper and Row.

Simpson, S. (2001) 'Working with children with written language difficulties', in Kersner, M. and Wright, J. A. (eds) *Speech and Language Therapy: The decision-making process when working with children*, 201–14. London: David Fulton Publishers.

Starkweather, C. W. and Gottwald, S. R. (1990) 'The demands and capacities model: II. clinical implications', *Journal of Fluency Disorders* **15**, 143–57.

Syder, D. (1992) *An Introduction to Communication Disorders.* London: Chapman and Hall.

Van Riper, C. (1982) *The Nature of Stuttering*, 2nd edn. New Jersey, USA: Prentice-Hall.

Verhulst, F. C. (1995) 'A review of community studies', in Verhulst, F. C. and Koot, H. (eds) *The Epidemiology of Child and Adolescent Psychiatry*, 146–77. Oxford: Oxford University Press.

Weitzman, E. (1992) *Learning Language and Loving It.* Toronto: Hanen Centre.

Wells, G. (1985) *Language Learning and Education.* Windsor: NFER Nelson.

Williams, D. (1995) *Early Listening Skills.* Bicester: Winslow Press/Speechmark.

Wood, D., Wood, H., Griffiths, A. and Howarth, I. (1990) *Teaching and Talking with Deaf Children.* Chichester: John Wiley & Sons.

Wright, J. A. and Kersner, M. (1998) *Supporting Children with Communication Problems: Sharing the load.* London: David Fulton Publishers.

Yairi, E. and Ambrose, N. G. (1999) 'Early childhood stuttering I: persistency and recovery rates', *Journal of Speech, Language and Hearing Research* **42**, 1097–112.

Useful Addresses

AFASIC
2nd Floor 50–52 Great Sutton Street
London EC1V 0DJ
www.afasic.org.uk

Blissymbols
The Blissymbol Resource Centre
ACE Centre
92 Windmill Road
Headington
Oxford OX3 7DR

The British Stammering Association
15 Old Ford Road
Bethnal Green
London E2 9PJ
(If writing please enclose s.a.e.)
www.stammering.org

British Sign Language
RNID
19–23 Featherstone Street
London EC1Y 8SL
www.rnid.org.uk

National Deaf Children's Society
15 Dufferin Street
London EC1Y 8UR
www.ndcs.org.uk

(For **Derbyshire Language Scheme**)
Mark Masidlover
Chief Educational Psychologist
Derbyshire Education Authority
Grosvenor Rd
Ripley DE5 3JE

The Hanen Centre
1075 Bay Street
Suite 403
Toronto
Ontario
M5S 2B1
Canada
www.hanen.org

Makaton + Makaton Symbols
Makaton Vocabulary Development Project
The Director
31 Firwood Drive
Camberley, Surrey
GU15 3QD
www.makaton.org

Index